WORD STRUCTURE

IN THE SAME SERIES

Editor: Richard Hudson

WORD STRUCTURE

Richard Coates

London and New York

First published 1999
by Routledge
11 New Fetter Lane, London EC4P 4EE

Simultaneously published in the USA and Canada
by Routledge
29 West 35th Street, New York, NY 10001

Typeset in Times Ten by
The Florence Group, Stoodleigh, Devon

Printed and bound in Great Britain by
TJ International Ltd, Padstow, Cornwall

British Library Cataloguing in Publication Data
A catalogue record for this book is available from the British Library

Library of Congress Cataloguing in Publication Data
A catalogue record for this book has been requested

ISBN 0–415–20631–6

CONTENTS

USING THIS BOOK

Some words are seamless. Many words are not just single chunks, but are made up of more than one bit. This book explores what can be said about their structure from several viewpoints, encouraging you to take an objective and analytic approach; to take words to pieces to see how they work as part of the system of the language they belong to. Their structure is one part of the fascination of words; Laurie Bauer explores other aspects of this fascination in his companion book to this one, *Vocabulary*.

In **Unit 1** we establish the basic fact that many words are divisible. **Units 2** and **3** explore what kinds of meanings their components might be capable of bearing. What is the difference between the ways *started* and *starter* can be divided up? In **Units 4** and **5**, we learn about a general classificatory system applicable to all languages: the solid framework of roots and bases, and the special modifications applied to that framework by the demands of grammar. This knowledge begins to be applied immediately in **Unit 6**, where some aspects of the word structure of two contrasting languages, Turkish and Latin, are analysed in detail. The work you do in this Unit mirrors exactly the way linguists go about their business: making hypotheses on the basis of data available so far, and then refining and improving the analysis as more and more data are added. **Unit 7** is a safari park in which you can see close up something of the exotic range of structures used by the languages of the world to build their words. In **Unit 8**, we return to English to look at one special part of that range, namely the many types of abbreviation, some of which may give birth to new words. **Units 9** and **10** are about the fact that even the building blocks of words don't always come in the same shape. Where does the -*f* go to when we make *loaf* into *loaves*?

Your way through the book is punctuated by exercises in the form of questions, the answers to which are printed at the back of the book (pages 83–97). Some of these are very easy, but they get harder as the Units progress. Most of these invite you to draw some conclusions from, and make an analysis of, some real data from a wide range of languages. We concentrate on English, but our data ranges from Papua New Guinea to the Central America of Columbus's time, and from East Africa to Siberia. After each question you should go to the answer before returning to the discussion in the text. Sometimes the 'answer' refers you directly back to the text for the discussion.

This book can't cover all the things which will catch your interest as you start your work in linguistics. Some of the questions which you are bound to raise are covered by other books in this series. Laurie Bauer's on *Vocabulary* was mentioned above; you will also enjoy Richard Hudson's books on *Word Meaning* and *English Grammar*, Nigel Fabb's on *Sentence Structure*, and Edward Carney's *English Spelling*. Changing patterns in language are explored by Jonathan Culpeper's book on the *History of English* and R. L. Trask's on *Language Change*.

Nothing is more fascinating than the workings of the one specialist precision tool that we all use – language. Use these books to analyse, understand and enjoy.

NOTE

SMALL CAPITALS will be used for a technical term on its first use or explanation, or when giving a significantly-placed reminder.

CAPITAL LETTERS are used for the names of lexemes (see **Unit 2**), except in data-sets.

Italics are used for word-forms (see **Unit 2**), except in data-sets.

'Single quotes' enclose meanings or glosses.

* is used sparingly to indicate a structure which is ill-formed.

ACKNOWLEDGEMENTS

I am deeply indebted to the series editor, Professor Richard Hudson, for his patience and guidance during the writing of this book, and to other scholars for discussion of some difficult points in languages in which they are specialists.

Much of the data is derived from the author's personal knowledge or public-domain information, and in some cases traditional analyses. Special acknowledgement is made here of intellectual debts regarding work on languages less well-known in Britain:

Agarabi: Jean Goddard
(Egyptian) Arabic: T. F. Mitchell
Basque: Larry Trask
Chamorro: Donald M. Topping
Chichewa: Mark Hanna Watkins
Fula: D. W. Arnott
Inuit: G. A. Menovshchikov
Korean: Samuel E. Martin
Koryak: A. N. Zhukova
Luganda: E. O. Ashton and others
Maasai: A. N. Tucker and J. Tompo ole Mpaayei
Maori: Andrew Carstairs-McCarthy
Nahuatl: J. R. Andrewes
St Lucia Creole: Lawrence Carrington
Tatar: M. Z. Zakiev
Yidiny: R. M. W. Dixon

The data collected by Menovshchikov and Zhukova is presented in Andrew Spencer, *Morphological theory* (Blackwell, 1991), but the use made of it here is my own.

Some of the Nahuatl data is taken from an exercise in Richard A. Demers and Ann K. Farmer, *A linguistics workbook* (MIT Press, 1986), but the use made of it here is my own.

One exercise is based on, but not identical to, a 'grapevine' data-set that I can no longer attribute to a particular originator. If an originator should be acknowledged, it will be done in any reprint of this book.

Workbooks in linguistics often invent languages to supply a ready source of tidy data. I have rejected this way of doing things, but I have occasionally slightly changed the facts of some real language to avoid a distracting complication. I don't think in any instance I have done serious violence to the structure of the language, and in any case I have usually signalled this. When specialists spot it happening, they should remember the purpose of the book.

Richard Coates
Falmer, Sussex, 23 July 1998

DIVIDING WORDS UP

An exploration of what it means for words to have parts.

Quite a lot of the material in this book assumes that you have some knowledge of the way the words of a language fall into groups, i.e. the traditional 'parts of speech' or LEXICAL CATEGORIES, such as noun, verb, adjective, preposition and so on. If you don't have this knowledge, some of the data presented in this Unit will introduce you gently to the idea that there are different types of word, and to the names that have been applied to these types.

Lexical categories

Many words in many languages are complete as they are. They don't obviously consist of smaller pieces. We'll start with English data (which will loom large in this book) and work on to other languages afterwards, where appropriate. Here are some English examples of one-piece words.

ONE-PIECE WORDS

> *Nouns*: tea machine pilchard shoulder duty kangaroo syllabus
> *Verbs*: steal exist possess harass develop astonish
> *Adjectives*: small bright new straight serene
> *Adverbs*: fast here soon ever often
> *Prepositions*: in with to about
> *Pronouns*: me them it you
> *Conjunctions*: and but or that while

Counting how many pieces a word has isn't the same as checking how many syllables a word has. The ones in the list above have anything from one to three syllables, and you can find some even longer words that seem complete in themselves:

Discussion

> didgeridoo   mulligatawny   abracadabra
> millennium   rhododendron

But we'll look later on at the question of whether some such words really do have constituent parts after all.

STRUCTURE

Morpheme

On the other hand, lots of words in all of these classes do evidently consist of smaller pieces – they have STRUCTURE. Each of the elements that you can divide a word into is technically called a MORPHEME, for reasons that I'll explain below. Here are some words with more than one of them.

> *Nouns*: teapot software flatfish tomcat placement breath-lessness normality
> *Verbs*: revalue dispossess threaten overdevelop auto-destruct
> *Adjectives*: dreadful streetwise carefree messy downcast
> *Adverbs*: strongly sometimes yesterday hereabouts
> *Prepositions*: into onto around upon
> *Pronouns*: anyone yourself nobody yous or youall (for speakers of some dialects)
> *Conjunctions*: however whereas unless

Discussion

Boundary

Most of these are quite obvious. Perhaps you had to think a bit about *threaten* and *around*, but if we were to write *threat-en* and *a-round*, with the BOUNDARY marked in as a hyphen, the point would be clear. The words are related to *threat* and *round*, and were coined out of them at some remote time in the past. Did you notice those ones with three morphemes? (*Breathlessness*, *normality*, *sometimes*, *hereabouts*.)

EXERCISE

1.1 Divide these words up into their constituent parts (morphemes):

> thickset bookshelf thinkable outbid   nowhere legless
> quickly rooms   outer   preview thinking unsafe

Discussion

That was easy in itself, and I won't spell out the answers. But the results are different in the two sets of words. Notice that when you divide up the words in the first line, on the face of it you get two pieces which are both in themselves English words: *thick* and *set*, *book* and *shelf*, and so on. When you divide up the words in the second line, you get an English word – *quick*, *room*, *out*, etc. – plus a bit that is clearly English but not a word – *-ly*, *-s*, *-er*, etc. These pieces cannot stand by themselves, and independence is one of the criteria for calling an element a word. Those elements that can stand

Free morphemes

by themselves as words are called FREE MORPHEMES; those that can't stand alone, but need the support of other morphemes, are called

Bound morphemes

BOUND MORPHEMES. But the overwhelming majority of morphemes, free or bound, have one or more meanings of their own. Typical morphemes are meaningful. That is part of the definition of the term for some analysts, though in due course we shall see some morphemes that don't have any meaning.

Notice that if you identify an element as a morpheme, in doing so you identify a position in a word into which other material – other morphemes – can be substituted: start with *out-bid*, and you can progress to *out-face, -sell, -do, -play, -smart, -live* and so on. In such constructions, the combinations of morphemes will often have similar types of meanings – here, all are verbs meaning roughly 'do something more or better than someone else'. There is not just a pattern, but a meaningful pattern.

Thinkable and *legless* deserve another look: notice that *-able* and *-less* aren't actually pronounced exactly like the ordinary words *able* and *less*. In fact, they don't mean the same either. *Able* doesn't have the same range of meanings as *-able;* people are able, but things can be *X*-able, as in *That information was not recoverable* or *This beer is quite drinkable*. Roughly speaking, *less* means 'not so much of', whilst *-less* means 'having none of'. This sort of fact makes us consider *-able* and *-less* to be *not* the words *able* and *less* themselves, but bound morphemes related to them. There is another instance of this sort of thing in exercise 1.4.

EXERCISES ✎

1.2 In this list of English words, pick out the free and bound morphemes:

showcase f	flashy b	started b	outworker f ، b
boxfile f	resistance b	sisterly b	distaste b
hurtful b	unbiased b ،	username f 3	engagement b
wrongdoing f 4	wizardry b	beaten b	insane f
volleyball f	brightness b	mortality b	perfection b
African b	upgrade f	commonest b	retrain b
unsafe b	hopelessly b 2	shown b	unbutton b
Jonathan's b	blockage f		

1.3 Notice that some of the words have more than two morphemes in them – for instance *outworker*. Which other four are absolutely clear instances?

- ful

1.4 Which example-word contains an element comparable with the *-able* and *-less* that were just discussed?

Discussion

Not many problems in this list. Perhaps you wondered whether *-ful* was free or bound, in *hurtful*. The answer is bound. It's not spelt like *full*, and if you consider its pronunciation carefully, it's not pronounced exactly like it either in most accents of English. Another consideration is that it doesn't *mean* 'full' either, though the two meanings aren't completely irrelevant to each other either. It means something to do with an association, strong or weak: 'characterized by (e.g. inspiring, promoting, possessing . . .) X', where X is the word that it is attached to. Compare:

dreadful	fearful	sinful	peaceful	painful
powerful	useful	tasteful		

This makes it like the *-able* and *-less* discussed above.

What it takes to be a morpheme

In all the material we've looked at so far, each of the morphemes we have picked out has a recognizable meaning. In *bookshelf*, both *book* and *shelf* are meaningful. In *unsafe*, both *un-* and *safe* are meaningful, though we have to recognize that *un-* has a meaning of an abstract sort: it contradicts or reverses the meaning of whatever follows (*un-safe* = 'not safe'; *un-button* = 'reverse the action called "button"'). In *thinking*, it's even harder to specify the meaning of the bound morpheme *-ing* without getting into grammatical technicalities. We'll do this later, but for the moment let's just note that one or more clear meanings really can be established for *-ing*.

The case for an element to be regarded as a morpheme is strengthened if it doesn't just exist within a single word, but recurs in others with a recognizably related meaning. When examining the credentials of any element, we should look for its recurrence elsewhere as corroboration.

A morpheme may be involved in regular patterns of interchange. For instance, *-est* in *longest* gains credibility as a morpheme not only because it's what is left over when you remove the meaningful *long*, but also because it interchanges with *-er* in a regular meaning-relationship found in hosts of other adjectives too (*softer*, *softest*; *duller*, *dullest* and so on). Those that behave like this are the ones that are most firmly integrated into the language-system.

Meaningfulness
Recurrence
Regular interchanges

Typical morphemes then (1) are MEANINGFUL, (2) RECUR in a language's vocabulary and (3) may recur in REGULAR INTERCHANGES.

We'll examine some apparent exceptions to (2) in **Unit 3** and elsewhere.

Some words happen to include strings of letters which have the same shape as recognizable morphemes, but which are clearly not true morphemes.

EXERCISES ✎

1.5 Compare the following pairs of words, and decide which consist of one morpheme and which of two.

baked	naked
printer	winter
killing	shilling
harden	garden
reheat	retreat

preview	precinct
sticker	flicker
undue	under
hardest	harvest
unstable	constable
cafeteria	wisteria

You may have some slight reservations about the solution offered. Perhaps you know, for instance, that many plant-names were formed by adding *-ia* to the name of a dead botanist, and you might correctly guess that that is the explanation for *wisteria*. So for some people, it might make sense to identify a bound morpheme *-ia* used in forming plant-names, which recurs in *dahlia*, *gloxinia*, *lobelia*, *alstroemeria* and so on. To get a fully meaningful division into morphemes you would then have to know or presume that Wister, Dahl, Gloxin, l'Obel and Alstroemer were botanists.

We shall see later (**Unit 3**) that words may consist *only* of bound morphemes. English examples are *hypothermia*, *presumption* and *exclude*, and the *mortality* that you met in exercise 1.2 above.

1.6 Which of the following English words are one-morpheme words? Remember that if you make a division each element that results should ideally be a recognizable piece of English – no loose ends allowed.

anorak	shovel	flower	cricket	placebo	artichoke
spider	little	booty	bootee	warmth	crackle

Most people, I'm sure, would want to recognize *boot* in *bootee*, because of the strong resemblance in meaning, but that leaves the problem of what to make of *-ee*. If you want to say it's a version of the *-y* (note the same pronunciation) found in *welly* or *pinny*, you have a stronger case for recognizing it. Sometimes a connection such as that seen in *boot/bootee* is so strong that analysts will accept it even at the cost of finishing up with an obscure piece. There is evidence that ordinary speakers of languages do the same. For some users, this piece *-ee* has been taken up and re-used in other much less well-known words such as *coatee* and *muffetee*, showing how a new morpheme might be created.

1.7 What might the morpheme *-ee*, if that's what it is, mean?

People often make the mistake of confusing the structure a word might once have had with the structure that it actually has, and think that its old structure represents its 'real' meaning. As language changes, structure may turn out not to be permanent. It would be hard to argue for the connection that once existed between *spanner* and *span*, for instance.

Don't let your knowledge of the words of other languages influence your analysis of expressions borrowed into English. Notice that *placebo* contains more than one morpheme in the language from which it has been borrowed – Latin – where it means literally 'I shall give pleasure' (*plac-e-b-o* roughly 'please – verb class II marker – non-present tense, imperfective aspect, active voice, indicative mood marker – 1st person singular non-past-tense marker'; don't worry if any of these terms are unfamiliar). It can't be said to have this structure in English, of course. Don't be caught out by such alien words as *gung-ho*, *karaoke*, *hara-kiri, cannelloni* and *nouveau-riche*. If they are completely segmentable into meaningful morphemes for you, then you know something about Mandarin Chinese ('work together', anglicized), Japanese (literally 'empty orchestra' and 'belly cutting'), Italian ('big stalks') or French ('new rich'). That isn't knowledge of English.

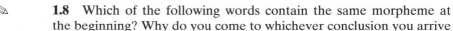

EXERCISE ✎

1.8 Which of the following words contain the same morpheme at the beginning? Why do you come to whichever conclusion you arrive at?

engulf	ennoble	ensconce	entangle	enrich
enthuse	envelop	entitle	encourage	encode
enhance	enlarge	enrage	entwine	entrust

Discussion

There is room to argue about the details of the solution. But at the very least, you need to note that some of these words cannot reasonably be subdivided into meaningful elements at all, e.g. *ensconce*, *enthuse*, *enhance* and probably *envelop*. The others all begin with a morpheme *en-*, but not necessarily the same one in all instances. Some of the *en-* morphemes make nouns into verbs, e.g. *enrage*, and some make adjectives into verbs, e.g. *enlarge*. Whether these really are the same element would take us too far afield to discuss at the moment. We'll examine some of the jobs done by individual morphemes in following Units.

Simple division into morphemes in languages other than English

Agarabi is a language of Papua New Guinea, of uncertain classification. The data is slightly simplified.

Agarabi

EXERCISE ✎

1.9 Identify the morphemes illustrated in this data. What exactly does each morpheme mean?

tinohe	'my mother'
anohe	'your mother'
anohe	'his or her mother'
tipohe	'my father'
apohe	'your father'
apohe	'his or her father'
tiro	'hit me'
aro	'hit him or her'
time	'give me'
ame	'give him or her'
ahnon	'his or her head'
amaah	'his or her house'
-tinta	'for me'
-anta	'for you'
-anta	'for him or her'

Maasai is a Nilo-Saharan language spoken in Kenya.

Maasai

1.10 Study the following nouns. If these words are typical, how do you form words denoting more than one of some object?

EXERCISE ✎

olkurruk	'crow'	ilkurruki	'crows'
olmeut	'giraffe'	ilmeuti	'giraffes'
olmeregesh	'ram'	ilmeregeshi	'rams'
olosowuan	'buffalo'	ilosowuani	'buffaloes'
enpoor	'stony place'	inpoori	'stony places'
endap	'palm of hand'	indapi	'palms of hand'
entasat	'old woman'	intasati	'old women'
entarakuet	'impala'	intarakueti	'impala (plural)'

Inuit is the language of the Inuit (Eskimos), Eskimo-Aleut family, spoken in Greenland, Canada, Alaska and Northern Russia.

Asiatic Inuit (Naukan dialect)

Exactly what sounds are denoted by the special symbols is not important for this exercise, except the fact that they are all consonants except ɨ, which is a vowel. The colon (:) means that the preceding vowel is long.

The meanings in English (due to Andrew Spencer) of the forms in this data are quite complex. The questions for you are simple, though:

1.11 What are the morphemes carrying the dictionary meaning ('work', 'walk', 'sleep', 'make holes', etc.)?

EXERCISES ✎

1.12   What is the morpheme meaning 'he or she', more fully and technically '3rd person singular, present tense', corresponding to English *-s* in *walks*, and so on?

aglukata:quq	'begins to work'
agluka:quq	'works with intermittent stoppages'
aglunani:ʁaquq	'stops working'
aglufqara:quq	'rarely works'
agluvrɨʁa:quq	'works with difficulty'
aqujgaquq	'wanders about'
aqujviluxtaquq	'walks back and forth'
iglɨχtɨpixtaquq	'walks a lot'
iglɨχtɨkʃa:ga:quq	'walks very slowly'
iglɨχtɨkjo:ʁaquq	'scarcely drags (oneself) along'
qɨɬpɨχta:quq	'makes holes in something'
qɨɬpɨχquʁa:quq	'makes holes in various places'
qavaχɬɨqja:quq	'sleeps fitfully'
qavaruga:quq	'sleeps soundly'
qavamse:quq	'dozes'
ku:jma:quq	'is swimming habitually towards . . .'
ku:jmaʁo:ʁaquq	'swims habitually'
ɬiŋaχtaquq	'rings'
ɬiŋaχtaga:taquq	'rings intermittently'

Discussion

The morpheme that carries the dictionary meaning, and on which these word-forms are built, comes at the beginning, and the third-person singular morpheme at the end in the shape *-quq*. The boundaries of these come at the point in each word where a common shape can be observed. So 'work' is *aglu-*, 'wander' is *aquj-*, and so on.

Morphological segmentation
Morphology

What you have done so far – dividing words up into morphemes – is called segmentation, or in its full technical splendour MORPHO-LOGICAL SEGMENTATION. The academic study of word structure is called MORPHOLOGY.

You can practice on the word itself: *morphology* is *morph-ology*, the second element meaning 'the academic study of', as in *psychology*, *biology* and so on. The first element is an adaptation of the Greek word μορφή meaning 'form' or 'shape'. It was also present in *morpheme*, of which I promised an explanation: *-eme* is an element invented for technical use by linguists, and means 'separate or distinctive unit of'. So a morpheme is a separate or distinctive unit of the form or shape of words. Words will tend to have structure for some purpose, which is why morphemes typically have a meaning of their own.

Morphology is not always as easy as in the examples presented so far. You may have had to think sometimes about whether to segment a word or not, but you have not had any significant problem with deciding where to segment once the decision to do it has been taken. We'll need to confront the questions of:

(i) what to do with obscure bits (**Unit 3**);
(ii) how to handle material where the same morpheme appears in different shapes.

OUTCOMES OF UNIT 1

Skills learnt

- segmentation into morphemes; identification of morphemes
- substitution as a test for being an element of a language

Terms learnt

LEXICAL CATEGORY (PART OF SPEECH); MORPHEME; FREE MORPHEME; BOUND MORPHEME; BOUNDARY; RECURRENCE; REGULAR INTERCHANGE; SEGMENTATION; MORPHOLOGY

Principles learnt

- Morphemes are typically meaningful units.
- Morphemes are typically recurrent units.
- Morphemes may form a system of interchangeable elements.

2 WORDS AND PARADIGMS

Exploring the ambiguity of the word *word* and some conse-
quences of this. Using organizing principles to show the relation
between pieces of data.

**WHAT IS A
WORD?**

So far we've been getting along without recognizing that the word
word is used in more than one way. There is a major ambiguity in
the term, and we must discuss it. We have to separate out the
concepts for which it is a label. Then, to ensure that we can analyse
data with precision in the Units that follow, we must introduce
technical terms for each of the relevant concepts.

**LEXEMES AND
GRAMMAT-
ICAL
WORD-FORMS**

Consider this; how many words are there in this sentence?

    Somebody donated a map because I like maps.

There are eight candidates for analysis; simply counting them is no
problem. But an important consideration in morphology is the fact
that the same vocabulary unit is not always represented by the same
form. Very often, these differences correspond to meaning differences
of a grammatical sort. Examine the separate, distinct word-forms
map and *maps*. Each of these represents the same vocabulary unit
or LEXEME in a rather subtle way. They differ in their grammatical
properties. *Map* is used, here, to refer to a single map, and *maps* to
every map. They differ, in the traditional terminology, in NUMBER, as
singular and plural form respectively. The basic dictionary notion of
map ('representation (usually in a plane diagram) of part of the
earth's surface') remains unaltered by this choice of number. They
are therefore different GRAMMATICAL WORD-FORMS of the same lexeme. There are therefore seven different lexemes represented in the
example-sentence.

Lexeme

**Grammatical
word-forms**

We have a notation for making this distinction: lexemes are written in capital letters, and grammatical word-forms in italics. So MAP in this discussion has the two word-forms *map* and *maps*. MAP is a name for the lexeme covering both the forms in which it appears. Take care to notice that MAP isn't the same as *map*.

I'll continue to use the word *word* when there is no serious possibility of misunderstanding, and to avoid being excessively technical. But remember this is only informal.

Lexemes fall into the traditional classes that we mentioned in **Unit 1** (noun, verb, adjective, preposition, and so on).

2.1 How many formally different grammatical word-forms does a typical English noun like ROOM or GIRL have? Try to think of all the different types of phrase in which you might use them.

Do you get different answers if you think of (a) the written and (b) the spoken forms separately?

2.2 How many different grammatical word-forms does a typical English verb like PLAY or SEEM have? Try to think of all the different types of phrase in which you might use them.

Do you get different answers if you think of (a) the written and (b) the spoken forms separately?

Discussion
Paradigm

The various grammatical forms of any given lexeme, when grouped together and organized, are called the PARADIGM of that lexeme.

If you are a user of standard written English, the paradigm of GIRL, as a written unit, consists of the forms *girl*, *girl's*, *girls* and *girls'*. We can set this information out according to its organizing principles of number and CASE, yielding a paradigm of four CELLS:

Cells

Paradigm of GIRL (written)

	singular number	plural number
non-possessive case	*girl*	*girls*
possessive case	*girl's*	*girls'*

Possessive case is the form used, as its name implies, to mark possession, as in *the girl's wardrobe* and *the girls' wardrobe*. For many current writers of English, this may be somewhat baffling, as there is a strong tendency to omit some or all apostrophes, disguising the difference between the possessive and the non-possessive forms. But what I have set out is standard, traditional, written English.

Is the paradigm of ROOM similar to that of GIRL? In principle, yes; but many people never use the possessive forms of nouns that denote inanimate objects. Would you say *the room's ceiling* or *the ceiling of the room*?

As for the spoken forms of GIRL, notice again that three of the four cells in the paradigm can be filled by the same form, the effect of which is exactly the same as missing out the apostrophes in the written paradigm given above. (By the way, that also explains why so many people find it so hard to know where to write apostrophes; the rule-book for standard English tells them to write the same spoken form in three different ways.)

(Attention: a different interpretation of the 'possessive case' material is possible; but what is presented here is traditional.)

The paradigm of the verb PLAY, as a written unit, consists of the forms *play, plays, played* and *playing*. We can set this information out according to its organizing principles, this time needing no cross-classification:

Paradigm of PLAY (written)

present simple	*play*
present 3rd person singular	*plays*
infinitive/imperative	*play*
past simple	*played*
present participle	*playing*
past/passive participle	*played*

The names given to the forms are the traditional ones. The spoken forms can be classified in the same way. SEEM behaves in the same way as PLAY. There are no catches as there are with the nouns. Some of the forms have two different labels. This is because there are verbs in English in which the present simple and the infinitive/imperative are different from each other, and also some where the past simple is different from the past/passive participle.

2.3 Can you think of at least one verb in each of these two less typical categories?

Paradigms may vary vastly in size from lexical category to lexical category. The English verb data including PLAY and your answers to Exercise 2.3 show this in a minor way. They may also vary in size from language to language. The paradigms of any Italian noun contain only two forms, its singular (e.g. *ragazzo*, 'boy') and its plural (e.g. *ragazzi*, 'boys') – with due allowance for those few words that have more than one plural form, which are ignored here. There is only one organizing principle, namely number, of which there are only two terms, singular and plural. But you could argue that all Italian verbs have at least 51 forms – too many to simply list here.

Typical English verbs by contrast have just four forms, as exemplified by PLAY above; and with one exception even no untypical verb has more than five.

2.4   The verb BEAT, in standard British English, has the forms *beat*, *beating*, *beaten* and *beats*.

How do they fit into a paradigm like that for the verb PLAY just set out? Do any more organizing principles or terms need to be introduced so that all the forms of BEAT can be accommodated?

2.5   The verb BE has the forms *be, being, been, am, is, are, was* and *were*.

How do they fit into a paradigm like that for the verb PLAY just set out? Do any more organizing principles or terms need to be introduced so that all the forms of BE can be accommodated?

BEAT goes like PLAY, except that, unlike PLAY, it has different forms for the past simple tense and the past/passive participle – at least in standard English (*I beat him at chess (yesterday)* / *I have beaten him at chess*; contrast *I played him at chess (yesterday)* / *I have played him at chess*). It has the same number of forms, organized by the same principles, but arranged differently into a paradigm. BE, on the other hand, has more forms than BEAT, as a simple count shows. It has all the extra forms mentioned in the discussion after the paradigm of PLAY (above). Some can be accommodated by extending principles we already need, for example, the distinction *was*/*were* is accounted for by number and person differences (*was* being singular, except 2nd person (you-form), and *were* plural) but extended in just this verb alone to the past tense. No other verb does this. But BE also needs a true extension to that organizing principle of person; it is the only verb in present-day English that has any special way of marking any second person form (*you*-form) as distinct from the first person.

Discussion

2.6   LATIN verbs are more complicated than English ones, and have a richer system of grammatical endings with some complexity inside them and some interpredictability. Here are some forms – only a small subset – from the paradigm of AUDIO ('hear'). Can you supply the missing forms? (Segment the forms into morphemes before you answer the question.)

person/number	'I hear', etc.	'I will have heard', etc.	'I was hearing', etc.
1 SG	audio	audivero	audiebam
2 SG	?aude	audiveris	audiebas
3 SG	audit	audiverit	?audiebat
1 PL	audimus	?audivermus	audiebamus
2 PL	auditis	?audiveris	?audiebaus
3 PL	audiunt	audiverunt	audiebant

The forms of a fourth 'tense' ('I may hear', etc.) are: *audiant*, *audias*, *audiamus*, *audiam*, *audiat* and *audiatis*. Which person/number does each of these represent?

Regular
Irregular

If the forms related in a paradigm fall into patterns with clear constructional principles, and if many other lexemes follow the same pattern, that paradigm is said to be REGULAR. PLAY is a regular verb. So is AUDIO. A paradigm is IRREGULAR if the constructional principles are more obscure and if a smaller number of lexemes follow it. BE is an irregular verb; in fact it's unique. Minor recurrent variants may be described as SUBREGULAR; there is a subregularity in English by which a verb may have an infinitive with the same form as the past tense. BEAT falls into this group, but more typical members of it are HIT, CUT and LET, which don't have a distinction between past simple and past/passive participle forms either (both being *hit*, *cut*, *let*).

Subregular

Filling in cells in paradigms: observing patterns and using their predictive power

Here are some verb-forms from the dialect of French spoken in Jersey. A set of forms for the verb CRAITHE ('to believe') is given. This time we have given traditional names to the 'tense'-forms, but the only important point here is to recognize that they are distinct in meaning from each other.

Jersey French

EXERCISES ✎

2.7 Can you fill in the corresponding forms for the other verbs?

CRAITHE 'to believe'
present tense, indicative mood

number	SG	PL
person		
1	*j'crai*	*j'criyons*
2	*tu crai*	*ou criyez*
3	*i'crait*	*i'craient*

present tense, subjunctive mood

number	SG	PL
person		
1	*j'craie*	*j'craithêmes*
2	*tu craies*	*ou craithêtes*
3	*i'craie*	*i'craient*

TRAITHE 'to milk'
present tense, indicative mood

number	SG	PL
person		
1	j'trai	j'triyons
2	?	?
3	?	i'traient

present tense, subjunctive mood

number	SG	PL
person		
1	j'traie	j'traithêmes
2	?	?
3	?	?

BRAITHE 'to bray'
present tense, indicative mood and number

number	SG	PL
person		
1	?	?
2	?	?
3	i'brait	i'braient

present tense, subjunctive mood

number	SG	PL
person		
1	?	?
2	?	ou braithêtes
3	?	?

2.8 If 'we used to milk' is *j'triyions*, what is 'we used to believe'?

2.9 If 'braying' is *briyant*, what is 'believing'?

2.10 The verb VAIE 'to see' is very similar. The 2nd person plural present subjunctive is *ou verrêtes*. What is the 1st person plural form?

2.11 The verb BAITHE 'to drink' is very similar. The 3rd person plural present subjunctive is *baivent*. What is the 2nd person plural form?

Some languages have co-existing regularities. As traditionally taught, French has three fully regular verb-classes: those with infinitives in -*er* like DONNER 'to give', those in -*ir* like SUBIR 'to undergo' and those in -*re* like TENDRE 'to stretch'.

Morphological class

Accordingly, not all Jersey French verbs have paradigms corresponding to the ones set out. It is quite normal to discover that within a particular lexical category there may be several different paradigms. Each of these is called a MORPHOLOGICAL CLASS. It is these morphological classes which may be described as regular, irregular or subregular (see above). The Jersey French forms in Exercise 2.7 make up a minor subregularity. It is not known, from the psychological point of view, whether the existence of such morphological classes serves any useful purpose for real people processing their language in everyday situations; but they are a recurrent feature of very many languages.

Italian

Here is some data from Italian demonstrating the existence of morphological noun-classes.

EXERCISES ✎

2.12   How many noun-classes are there in Italian? (Remember: every different pattern of forms making up a paradigm makes a different morphological class. Group these nouns according to the way their singular and plural forms are related.)

singular	plural	meaning
bottiglia	*bottiglie*	'bottle'
ragazzo	*ragazzi*	'boy'
uovo	*uova*	'egg'
mano	*mani*	'hand'
stanza	*stanze*	'room'
legge	*leggi*	'law'
canzone	*canzoni*	'song'
psichiatra	*psichiatre*	'psychiatrist'
idiota	*idioti*	'idiot'
cuscino	*cuscini*	'pillow'
mattone	*mattoni*	'brick'
psichiatra	*psichiatri*	'psychiatrist'
lume	*lumi*	'lamp'
labbro	*labbra*	'lip'
lira	*lire*	'lira'
dito	*dita*	'finger'
quadro	*quadri*	'picture'
idiota	*idiote*	'idiot'
poema	*poemi*	'poem'

Discussion
Gender

These morphological classes aren't the same as genders. The GENDER of a noun is defined by what pronoun(s) may substitute for phrases containing it, and by patterns of agreement within such phrases. In Italian, agreement and substitution patterns exist, but they do not follow the five-way classification that you've just discovered. Instead, the traditional gender categories masculine and feminine cross-cut the noun-classes.

The form we use to name the paradigm we are observing – the one for which we use the CAPITALIZATION notation – is called the CITATION-FORM. In English, it looks fairly easy to decide what is the citation-form (remember how we chose MAP above). For the verb which has amongst its forms *stretch*, the infinitive form with *to*, TO STRETCH, is the citation-form (this is the word TO plus the most basic form of STRETCH – i.e. the one with no other morphemes attached), not the other possibilities *stretches*, *stretched* or *stretching*. Other languages don't always agree with English on which form to choose for this job. In French, as in English, you refer to a verb using its (in French, one-word) infinitive form: the verb AIMER is named using *aimer* ('to love'), for instance, not *aimons* ('(we) love') or *aimaient* ('(they) used to love'). But in Latin, the first person singular form of the present tense, indicative mood, active voice was used (AMO from *amo* ('I love')). In Basque, verbs are cited using the form called the perfective participle, because it is structurally the simplest form. So corresponding to TO LOVE is MAITATU, though *maitatu* actually means, in use, 'loved' as in 'I have loved'.

Citation-form

2.13 What is the citation-form of the English verb which has the following different grammatical word-forms: *am*, *are*, *be*, *been*, *being*, *is*, *was*, *were*?

EXERCISE ✎

Bear in mind that being identical in sound, spelling or both is not sufficient to prove that two word-forms represent the same lexeme. (TO) BEAR, for instance, may be a verb meaning 'carry' (among other things), or a noun denoting an animal. The two lexemes are each represented by a different array of word-forms (paradigm).

2.14 Even two closely-related items may be different lexemes. Using the criteria you just used for the two *bear*s, you should be able to establish easily that (TO) SMELL as a noun (*a nasty smell*) and a verb (*I can smell it*) is two different lexemes, because they are

EXERCISE ✎

represented by different arrays of word-forms. Which? List the relevant forms.

SMELL (noun):   (TO) SMELL (verb):

Discussion

Some, but not all, dictionaries will give separate entries to paired items of this kind; all will at least cross-reference them to each other, to take note of the fact that they are related in meaning despite their differences of behaviour with respect to their grammatical word-forms.

2.15 Revision exercise: how many lexemes appear in each of the following examples? In how many grammatical word-forms do each of the lexemes appear?

(a) Did you have measles before I had it?
(b) A half for me and two halves for these gentlemen.
(c) I can't stand having to stand on the bus.
(d) I was a student, then my daughter was, and now my son is.
(e) Sue has her likes and dislikes, but she knows what she likes, like anyone else.

OUTCOMES OF UNIT 2

Skills learnt

- pattern recognition: drawing up paradigms and using them to predict corresponding forms in the same morphological class
- judging whether paradigms are similar or different, and therefore whether they represent distinct classes
- thinking of examples to illustrate patterns
- classifying linguistic forms using the terms LEXEME, WORD-FORM.

Terms learnt

LEXEME; GRAMMATICAL WORD-FORM (for convenience often just WORD-FORM or even FORM); PARADIGM; REGULAR, IRREGULAR, SUBREGULAR; MORPHOLOGICAL CLASS; CITATION-FORM

Grammatical notions such as NUMBER, PERSON, TENSE and MOOD are mentioned, as are names for FORMS like IMPERATIVE, INFINITIVE and PARTICIPLE. But they are not fully defined here. Many are covered in David Crystal's book *Rediscover Grammar* (Longman, 1988).

Principles learnt

- The term WORD is ambiguous and needs to be supplemented by more technical ones.
- Lexical classes may be subdivided into groups of words (lexemes) with differing paradigms: morphological classes.

LEXICAL AND GRAMMATICAL MORPHOLOGY

3

> The different types of jobs that morphemes perform within a word

LEXICON AND GRAMMAR

Consider the word *actors*. What can you say about it in the light of what you've learned in **Units 1** and **2**? Clearly it's analysable into three morphemes, *act*, *-or*, *-s*. But they don't all have the same status; they don't do the same kind of job. The *-s* is the kind of element discussed in **Unit 2**. It reflects the category of NUMBER; it means 'plural'. *Actors* can therefore be analysed as a GRAMMATICAL WORD-FORM of the LEXEME ACTOR. This ACTOR is itself related to the lexeme ACT; adding the -OR converts this verb into a noun with the meaning 'performer of the action mentioned'. There will be more to say about these matters in the Units that follow. But the fundamental point here is that some morphology has to do with the internal structure of lexemes, as with ACT-OR, and some has to do with the internal structure of the forms that those lexemes may take, as with *actor-s*.

The principles by which grammatical word-forms can be structurally analysed belong to the GRAMMAR. The process that gives us *actors* is used to build word-forms of countless other lexemes. Processes like this are called INFLECTION or GRAMMATICAL MORPHOLOGY, and collectively they build up the PARADIGMS of lexemes (see **Unit 2**).

grammar

**Inflection
Grammatical
morphology**

EXERCISE

3.1 Can you think of any word-forms which appear to have a clear final *-s* morpheme but have no singular form?

Lexicon

Derivation

Lexical morphology

The principles by which lexemes can be analysed structurally belong to the LEXICON or vocabulary. The process that gives us ACTOR is used in the structure of lots of other lexemes too. Processes like this are called DERIVATION or LEXICAL MORPHOLOGY.

EXERCISE ✎

3.2 (a) Give six nouns ending in -OR where the relation between the noun and the verb to which it is added is as simple and clear as with ACT-OR.

(b) Did you come across any nouns with the same structure but with other sorts of meaning?

(c) Did you come across any nouns ending in -OR that denote human beings but aren't built on a verb in any obvious way?

DIFFERENCES BETWEEN LEXICAL AND GRAMMAT- ICAL MORPHEMES IN GENERAL

One significant difference between grammatical and lexical morphemes is that grammatical ones, like *-ed* in *threaded*, never change the category of the word they are attached to; that's trivial and it follows logically from their definition, which is 'markers of grammatical forms of some given lexeme'. Lexical ones, like -FUL in SPITEFUL and -ISH in WARMISH, may do. (In the case of SPITEFUL this actually happens; a noun is made into an adjective. In the case of WARMISH it doesn't; an adjective is made into an adjective.)

Another significant difference is that grammatical morphemes are in the overwhelming majority of cases bound, not free. Lexical morphemes may be either bound or free.

But the most important thing of all is that the products of lexical material are all themselves just lexemes. WRITER and SHOWER-GEL are nouns just like the simple PEN and SOAP. INTIMIDATE is a verb just like the simple SCARE. DOLEFUL is an adjective just like the simple SAD. Whatever can be added by way of extra morphemes to one member of these pairs can be added to the other (*writers/pens*, *shower-gels/soaps*, *intimidated/scared*, *dolefully/sadly*, *etc.*).

EXERCISES ✎

3.3   Which morphemes in the following words are lexical and which are grammatical?

(*Reminder*: removing grammatical material does not affect the lexical meaning of the word you are analysing. Removing the *-s* of *actors* leaves you with a different form, *actor*, of the lexeme ACTOR; removing the -OR gives you the distinct lexeme ACT. ACT and ACTOR have distinct paradigms, whilst *actor* and *actors* belong to the same paradigm.)

sparkler	benighted	detective	tympani
speeding	straightest	platypus	partly
threaded	oxen	disharmony	ghastlier
horsebox	embolden	two-handed	servant

Discussion

Speeding is ambiguous; the *-ing* is lexical in *Speeding is an offence* (where SPEEDING is a noun) and grammatical in *She was speeding on the motorway* (where *speeding* is a form of the verb SPEED). You can't tell what *-ed* is automatically. It's grammatical in *You've threaded your needle*, but lexical in *benighted*; there isn't a verb BENIGHT that it could be a form of. Much the same goes for TWO-HANDED. It's customary to treat the comparative *-er* in *ghastlier* and the superlative *-est* in *straightest* as grammatical. *Platypus* has lexical structure only for those who know its origins, and there is no grammatical material in it.

In English, where a word-form contains both lexical and grammatical morphemes, their order is fixed. Grammatical morphemes can only come after the STEM (discussed in **Unit 4**). So, based on *ox* and *speed*, you find *oxen* and *speeding*, but nothing analogous to **enox* or **ingspeed*. It follows from that that all grammatical morphemes follow any lexical morphemes; we have *act-or-s* but nothing like **act-s-or*.

An apparent exception:

3.4 The plural of COURT-MARTIAL for some users of English is *courts-martial*. The grammatical *-s* appears in the middle of the string of lexical morphemes. How can this be explained, or explained away?

Discussion

The simplest way of avoiding the problem is to say that COURT-MARTIAL is a phrase, not a word. If, on the other hand, you say *court-martials*, there is nothing to stop you claiming that COURT-MARTIAL is a multi-part lexeme; the grammatical morpheme is where it's expected to be in a word-form.

BOUND LEXICAL MORPHEMES

Many of the morphemes you can identify by analysis are not independent, and are related in particular ways to the rest of the word which they make up. That's obvious for the grammatical morphemes that we've met. Let's now examine some lexemes which, for various reasons, are harder to segment and interpret convincingly than most of those that we've seen so far.

EXERCISES ✎

3.5 Can you segment these words?

linguist	utilize	arrogant	alacrity	biology
terrify	location	mechanic	democrat	meditate

3.7   What other evidence would lead you to have faith in the view that UTIL-, -FLECT and MEDIT- are morphemes?

Discussion

The key notions are those of RECURRENCE and INTERCHANGE that we introduced in **Unit 1**. If elements recur, and engage in interchange which seems to respect the element's meaning, you have a strong case for identifying them as linguistic elements that you would want to call morphemes.

Two procedures

Use your own knowledge of the English that you use – whatever you can call to mind with not too much thought – and then use a good dictionary, such as *OED*, *Collins* or *Longmans*, to discover further lexemes containing these elements. This will give you insight into two possible sorts of solution: one appropriate for you as a real user, and one for an idealized 'perfect' or 'optimal' user of English.

Discussion

There's obviously a reason to start by identifying an element such as -ATE as a morpheme; it has a verb-forming function in words like HYPHENATE, URIN(E)ATE, IMPERSONATE, LIQUIDATE and CONSOLIDATE. What it is added to in these words looks like a free morpheme of English. Much more usually, however, what it's added to is bound, as in FASCINATE, CELEBRATE, POSTU-LATE, EMULATE and of course MEDITATE.

Bound lexical morphemes are on a kind of gradient of reality: some occur more freely than others. Some are easier to justify than others. A justification would be based on the patterns of recurrence and interchange in which they participate, and the robustness of a single meaning over the whole range of lexemes including them.

3.8   What support is there for the existence of morphemes -MONGER, -SUME, -JECT, and what do they mean (if you conclude that they are real)?

Bound lexical morphemes, as we've noted, belong to no lexical cate-gory. They are only building-blocks used in the construction of more elaborate words, in parallel with elaborate ones built around free morphemes. It may be hard to specify their precise dictionary meaning since they do not occur as free morphemes and are not fully interchangeable with any which are free. They can't go every-where that free ones can go. There are plenty that recur more freely than the troublesome ones we've just been looking at, so we can move on positively. Take PSYCH-, as in PSYCHOLOGY, PSYCHI-ATRY or PSYCHOSIS. This is what's left over after you've taken away such clearly meaningful bound morphemes as -OLOGY ('acad-emic study of X'), -IATRY ('clinical treatment of X') and -OSIS ('pathological condition affecting X'). Well, what does PSYCH-mean – perhaps '(something to do with) the mind'? The answer appears to be: 'Yes, but only when the element combines with others.' It can't freely substitute for *mind* or *the mind* in ordinary English (you can't say: *'It completely slipped my psych-*). Very often such units recur with a whole range of other bound lexical morphemes or with bound derivational morphemes. For PSYCH-with -OLOGY and so on, compare NEUR- in NEUROLOGY, NEUROSIS, NEURITIS, and HAEMAT- in HAEMATOLOGY, HAEMATOMA, HAEMATURIA.

EXERCISES ✎   **3.9**   Identify the bound lexical morphemes in initial position in the following data. Can you confidently say what they mean?

pornography	histogram
bovine (compare equine, ovine, canine, feline)	leucocyte
medical	android
geriatric	regulate
horrify	theocracy

Discussion   BOVINE poses an interesting problem. -INE is clearly an adjective-forming morpheme meaning 'to do with (animal) X', as the other words given indicate. Having taken that off, you're left with *bov-*. This occurs in no other words, but is widely understood as 'to do with cattle'. That understanding is a sufficient justification for accepting BOV- as a bound lexical morpheme.

It looks as though it recurs in the trade-name *Bovril*, a brand of beef extract. That might be how the name is currently perceived, but its origin is actually different.

PORN(O)- occurs in no other words, except those based on PORNOGRAPHY, but has acquired independent status of its own as a noun (PORN) or an adjective (PORNO). That justifies it as a unit – perhaps not even bound any more. The same is true of MEDIC ('medical student, doctor'), if this is not perceived as just an abbreviation. The boundaries between elements may thus vary in strength over time.

Now consider the following:

3.10   Identify the bound morphemes below. Can you confidently say what they mean? If you are confident, explain why.

autoimmune	cruciform
gigabyte	television
millisecond	perinatal
hemisphere	manuscript
bibliomania	

In these words, the bound morphemes combine with free morphemes.

Discussion

Notice that elements like these very often participate in quite large systems of words. BIBLIO- alternates with other elements in naming other sorts of MANIA, and other fractions of seconds are named with elements other than MILLI-. BIBLIO- also combines with other elements like -GRAPHY and -PHILE; MILLI- also names fractions of other units like GRAMMES, LITRES, BARS and AMPERES.

Almost all bound lexical morphemes of this type, locked into quite complex systems of words, are of Greek or Latin origin. In a sense, they work as a kind of parallel vocabulary, a resource for the creation of words for special purposes, especially scientific and technical. They may be transparent for some users who have specialist knowledge, and not for others. ANGIOPLASTY may in effect be a single-morpheme item for non-specialists; specialists may see ANGIO-PLASTY '(blood-)vessel moulding'.

3.11   Predict the meaning of words invented from such bound lexical morphemes, using your knowledge of other words of English:

cardio- ('heart'):   cardiophobia, cardiectomy
gyneco- ('woman'): gynecophily, gynecandry, gynecocracy
hydro- ('water'):   hydroscopy, hydrometry

Some bound morphemes have no other function but to distinguish different types of whatever is indicated by some other morpheme in the word. An instance is afforded by names of berries in English – we find RASPBERRY, CRANBERRY, BILBERRY and most of the lexemes in this group have such an obscure element in them. CRAN- here has no meaning except 'type of berry'. Those morphemes which have only the meaning 'type of X' are in fact called CRANBERRY MORPHEMES after this famous example.

Cranberry morphemes

OUTCOMES OF UNIT 3

Skills learnt

- identifying lexical and grammatical elements
- finding parallels or analogues for given structures
- identifying patterns of derivation with free and bound elements
- interpretation of words created from bound elements

Terms learnt

LEXICON and GRAMMAR; LEXICAL and GRAMMATICAL INFORMATION; LEXICAL and GRAMMATICAL MORPHEMES; INFLECTION and DERIVATION; BOUND LEXICAL MORPHEMES; CRANBERRY MORPHEMES

Principles learnt

- The lexicon and the grammar contribute different kinds of meanings to a word.
- Lexical morphemes make up lexemes.
- Grammatical morphemes distinguish different word-forms of lexemes.
- Lexical items undergo grammatical processes (inflection) in the same way no matter how complex their own structure is.
- Meaningful elements need not be free.

Topic further practised

- segmentation and classification

ROOTS, BASES, STEMS AND OTHER STRUCTURAL THINGS

4

> Categorizing morphemes in terms of their relations with others in the same word; the sequence of elements and hierarchies of dependency.

ROOTS

When we look at words that have some internal structure, we may decide that the elements they consist of are not all equal: that some are more central than others. In *sending*, for instance, we see the structure *send-ing* and conclude that the free morpheme *send* has had the bound morpheme *-ing* attached after it, and not vice versa. In the case of *unjust*, we conclude something similar, but with the free and bound morphemes in the opposite order. *Un-* has been added to *just*, and placed in front of it. The key element to which others are added is called the ROOT of the word.

Root

EXERCISES

4.1 Can you identify the roots of the following words?

hymns	breakage	insane	majority	grandly
subhuman	outbreak	linked	boarder	renew

4.2 More than one additional element is possible. Can you identify the roots of these even more complex words?

knowingly	untainted	unreheated	insufferable
brainlessness	actions	rediscover	disinherited
ministerially	paranormality		

Discussion

Since they are morphemes, roots in principle have a lexical (dictionary) meaning. This is obvious in instances such as HYMN and

BREAK, KNOW and TAINT in these exercises. For some roots, however, those consisting of BOUND LEXICAL MORPHEMES (see **Unit 3**) such as LINGU- in LINGUIST and ARROG- in ARROGANT, we may have to say that they have a full meaning only when joined to other elements. These bound lexical morphemes may not be fully real for all speakers of the language being investigated: it depends how strongly they perceive the boundaries between the morphemes.

ROOTS AND NON-ROOTS

Bound derivational morphemes

The other elements which are not roots come in two different sorts. There are those that are used to express grammatical meanings, a concept which you met in the discussion of grammatical word-forms and paradigms in **Unit 2** and called GRAMMATICAL MORPHEMES. And there are BOUND DERIVATIONAL MORPHEMES which are used to form new, or derived, lexemes, i.e. further units with dictionary meanings of their own, as seen in earlier units. Some bound derivational morphemes appear in the words below; can you identify them?

EXERCISES ✎

4.3 Revision question: Identify the morphemes below which are used to form derived lexemes.

warmth   passage   accountable   prosperity endanger
dissection neutralize smithy   hearty   consultant
preschool buffoonery

4.4 In the first two data-sets in this unit, which of the elements are *not* being used to form derived lexemes (further words with different dictionary meanings from that of the root)? In other words, which are grammatical morphemes?

Discussion

The only grammatical morphemes are *-s* in *hymns* and the *-ed* seen in *linked* and *disinherited*. These do not provide further dictionary words, but add grammatical meanings to existing dictionary words. *-s* has to do with plurality, in this case 'more than one of what is specified, i.e. HYMN', and *-ed* has to do with either past tense or completion of action, here 'past tense or completion of the specified state or action LINK, DISINHERIT'. They form grammatical word-forms of the three lexemes mentioned.

ROOT, BASE, STEM AND AFFIX
Affixes, Base

The additional elements such as we have been examining in this Unit and previous ones, which we'll now call AFFIXES, are not independent. They are added to other elements. Whatever you can add affixes to is called a BASE. All roots are potentially bases (but not vice versa).

A base can be a plain root (e.g. SWITCH, BOTTLE, VANILLA) or more than one plain root (BELL-JAR, WINDOW-SEAT). A base can also consist of a root plus one or more affixes (CORNY, EX-HUSBAND). The most highly structured bases may consist of more than one base, one or each of which may be (a) a root equipped with affixes (STAND-OFFISH, DANO-NORWEGIAN, BLUEY-GREEN, RUMPY-PUMPY), or (b) a base which itself consists of multiple bases (RAILWAY STATION, ICE-CREAM SALESMAN).

Remember that not all affixes are lexical (i.e. they do not all form separate dictionary words) – some are grammatical. What you add grammatical affixes to is called a STEM, whether it is simple or complex in its own structure. A stem is therefore a special kind of base. All stems are bases, but not all bases can be stems in English because some lexical categories (e.g. prepositions) don't take grammatical affixes.

Stem

ROOT:	morpheme on which the rest of a word is built
BASE:	any structure to which an affix may be added
STEM:	any base to which a grammatical affix may be added
AFFIX (1):	LEXICAL affixes form separate dictionary words by being attached to bases (process: derivation) – see especially **Unit 3**.
AFFIX (2):	GRAMMATICAL affixes add grammatical meanings to the meaning of their stems (process: inflection) – see especially **Unit 2**.

Summary table

Linguists are not always consistent in their usage of the terms *root*, *base* and *stem*. I have presented what I think is the most widely accepted terminology for analysing word-structure, but you may find different accounts in other linguistics books.

Cautionary note

Study these worked examples, and then decide what the roots, bases, stems, lexical affixes and grammatical affixes in the words in the exercise that follows them are.

crow	base consisting of a single root; stem. That it can serve as a stem is shown by the next item.
crows	base consisting of a single root; stem plus grammatical affix.
crowbar	base consisting of two roots; stem. That it can serve as a stem is shown by the next item.
crowbars	the stem of the last item plus grammatical affix.
minority	base consisting of root plus lexical affix. Since you could have a form like *minority's* in *for the minority's sake*, it is also the stem of that.
gentlemanly	base consisting of two roots, plus lexical affix, making a more complex base. You can't add grammatical affixes to this, so it never serves as a stem. It does if you accept as an English word the superlative form *gentlemanliest*.

Examples

southernmost	base consisting of root plus lexical affix, to which a further lexical affix is added, making a more complex base. Again, not a stem, because you can't add any grammatical affixes to it (try!).
deserted	base consisting of a root; this base is also a stem to which a grammatical affix is added (assuming this to be the past tense of the verb TO DESERT).
Irish-American	base consisting of two bases, each consisting of a root plus a lexical affix. (The first root is a bound lexical morpheme seen also in *Ire-land*.) This base can serve as a stem, because you can add grammatical affixes to it (*Irish-Americans*).

Answer questions 4.5 to 4.8, using the data which follows them.

EXERCISES ✎

4.5 Give three examples of bases which are an element of one of the lexemes mentioned but aren't roots.

4.6 Give two examples of grammatical affixes.

4.7 Which word has two lexical affixes in succession?

4.8 Which words consist entirely of roots and/or affixes which are bound morphemes?

outgrow	presently	quicksilver	bathrooms
manhandled	gastritis	many-faceted	sleepyhead
truthfulness	bricklayer	reinvent	squeamish
headbanger	misstatement	hyperactive	browbeaten
agriculture	ludicrous		

DOING IT WITHOUT AFFIXES

Some lexemes may belong to different lexical categories without having that relationship marked in any way in their structure. As we saw above in **Unit 2**, SMELL may be a noun or a verb, and the differences appear only when they are modified for grammatical reasons – *smelled* can only be the form of a verb, though *smells* could be either a verb-form or a noun-form, with quite radically different meanings in each instance. Other instances of noun-verb pairs include DRINK, LOVE, DRIVE, REVIEW, DESPAIR and REQUISITION. Pairs of lexemes related in this sort of way are called CONVERSIONS; but it isn't always easy to form a view about which of the pair is converted into which.

Conversions

4.9 How exactly do you know which of the noun–verb pairs are verbs and which are nouns? What extra information would clinch the analysis, if it's not available in the data-set?

Verb	Noun
I drink beer	Beer is my drink
She loves you	She's in love with you
Let's drive	Let's go for a drive
I reviewed the situation	I prepared a review of the situation
I despair of you	I'm in despair about you
The gunners requisitioned the truck	The gunners put a requisition on the truck

Other pairs are related in a different way again: they are spelt alike but differ in pronunciation.

4.10 Consider CONVICT, EXPORT, REFIT, PROTEST and INCREASE, and establish that each of them may be pronounced in two different ways. What's the most striking difference between them? What meaning does the difference represent? Is this difference regularly present?

Discussion

The answer given represents what's usual – some speakers are not entirely consistent in all such words. Many Americans, for instance, use PRÓTEST as a verb, and I have regularly heard ÉXPORT as a verb in England. Some lexemes, such as DISPUTE, are members of this class for some speakers and not for others: some people say DISPÚTE for the noun (like the verb) and others DÍSPUTE.

4.11 Make a list of six words in English which can be either verbs or nouns without shifting of the stress, and a list of six further verbs and nouns related by shifting of the stress.

Where a base itself consists of two or more bases side by side as sisters, as in the case of COMPOUND LEXEMES (more on which in **Unit 5**), a hierarchy or relation of dependency usually exists between them. A HANDBAG is a sort of BAG. BAG is therefore the central element in the construction, and is therefore the HEAD; HAND is the DEPENDENT. Heads often occupy second place in English compounds.

Head
Dependent

It's obvious that a head will normally be of the same lexical category as the compound itself, as in these examples:

pathway   (noun)
name-call (verb)

blackmail	(noun and verb)
undercook	(in both the senses 'to leave partly raw' (verb) and 'subordinate cook' (noun))
househunt	(verb)
headstrong	(adjective)
within	(preposition)

Endocentric

This sort of compound is called ENDOCENTRIC ('having the centre inside'). But not all compounds can be sensibly analysed as 'sort of whatever the head is'. RED-EYE (the technical problem in photography) isn't a sort of eye, but EYE in RED-EYE is, like EYE by itself, a noun, so the condition for its being the head of the compound appears to be satisfied. But the semantic or meaning-head is unexpressed: the meaning of RED-EYE is something like 'result of poor technique showing up as red eyes in snapshots', and the head of this phrase is RESULT. The head is therefore, from this point of view, outside the expression being analysed. This sort of compound is

Exocentric

called EXOCENTRIC ('having the centre outside') – the meaning of the head is not directly expressed in the compound. It means a result to do with eyes, and RESULT is unexpressed.

Notice that BLACKMAIL can be a verb. Since MAIL accompanied by a dependent adjective can only be a noun, it's best to analyse BLACKMAIL as a noun of which MAIL is the head, and treat the verb as a conversion of the noun (see above).

Where the compound and the root of one of its bases do not share the same lexical category, even allowing for conversion, it isn't clear that it's appropriate to speak in terms of constructions with heads at all. Examples of this kind include EYEBRIGHT (the name of a plant), the pronoun SOMEBODY, MID-OFF (a fielding position in cricket) and HANGDOG (an adjective, as in a *hangdog look*).

EXERCISES ✎

4.12 Which of the following below are compounds? Of those that are, what is the head?

4.13 Which of the compounds are endocentric and which exocentric? (*Hint*: decide first whether to treat any of the examples as conversions.)

4.14 Which of the compounds are neither endocentric nor exocentric, but appear to have bases neither of which is dependent on the other, like for instance OAK-HAZEL in *oak-hazel woodland* ('woodland dominated by both oak and hazel')?

lockjaw	island	blackout	babysit
sisterhood	oversleep	actor-producer	lightweight
shortcrust	father-figure	sleepover	spring-clean

sit-in	grey-green	superstar	bread winner
evergreen	into		

Head-and-dependent structures of this kind are very important when words are first coined, but lexemes consisting of more than one element may lose their internal structure as time passes. For instance, meanings may go their own way: a STARFISH is not a fish, even though it was once considered to be one. FAR-FETCHED means 'implausible', the relevance of its parts and the way they fit together probably not being considered by people as they use it. MILDEW was once a compound, but nearly all trace of the fact has been lost.

Discussion

OUTCOMES OF UNIT 4

- establishing formal relatedness between words of different shape
- recognizing asymmetrical relationships among morphemes within a word

Skills learnt

ROOT; BASE; STEM; AFFIX; (bound) GRAMMATICAL MORPHEME; BOUND DERIVATIONAL MORPHEME; CONVERSION; HEAD; DEPENDENT; ENDOCENTRIC and EXOCENTRIC COMPOUND

Terms learnt

- Not all morphemes are of equal status in a word.
- Structure within a word is linear and hierarchical.

Principles learnt

- identification of morphemes fulfilling particular roles

Topics further practised

5 COMPOUND AND COMPLEX BASES

Analysing more deeply lexemes with elaborate internal structure.

RECAP

Stems are bases to which affixes with grammatical meanings – grammatical affixes – are attached. But bases themselves may show internal structure. The most obvious cases are those in which the base consists of two bases, both roots of which are free morphemes, in a head-dependency relation:

> houseplant password oversight bighead bootleg

Where the present-day English written form includes a hyphen we may also identify the items as being structured in the same sorts of ways as the set above:

> cross-stitch no-one brand-new London-bound
> phone-booth mob-law

(Not everyone will agree on whether or not to hyphenate some particular expression. That's not important here – it's a matter of spelling, not morphology.)

You might also say that some bases consisting of two elements where no hyphen is written are also structured in the same way, because of a special feature of their pronunciation: they are pronounced with their main stress on the first element, just like words of the HOUSEPLANT type, and they function just like them in sentences too.

> language expert history course tree surgeon
> learned society hockey stick mastic gun
> Santa Claus (if you're American)

(Not everyone will agree on whether to hyphenate some particular expression or leave a space. Don't worry about that here either. You will always be able to find other examples that satisfy you.)

They fit into sentences in the same way as the HOUSEPLANT type:

> That houseplant looks close to death.

> That language expert looks close to death.

Lexemes of this type, with stems consisting of two or more free-standing bases, are called COMPOUND LEXEMES.

Compound lexemes

5.1 English forms compounds very freely; many are in everyday use and many are created on the fly in conversation. Can you think of six compounds that have BOOK as the first element (e.g. BOOK-MARK) and six that have it as the second (e.g. SCRAPBOOK)?

EXERCISE ✎

The general meaning of compound bases is often very much harder to pin down precisely than that of complex bases, which are built using morphemes which aren't full words (see page 22). Most often, the best that can be said about compounds is that the two bases, and their meanings, are simply associated with each other. A good example is afforded by English words in -MAN.

milkman	dustman	doorman	houseman
postman	taxman	fisherman	gunman

Even restricting ourselves like this to [dependent noun + head noun] compounds, all meaning 'male person practising a trade or profession', we find no consistent relationship between the elements such that we can say the structure has some general meaning irrespective of which bases occupy the two slots. It isn't possible to say anything more about the structure of the compound MILKMAN than that it associates MAN (head) with MILK (dependent) in some way, and that the sense of MAN is modified or restricted by that of MILK in some way. The characteristic meaning, 'man who delivers milk to homes', is due to the particular bases which are compounded together here, not in any way to the structure [base + base]. There are plenty of other ways in which a man could be associated with milk – he could draw it from the cow, pasteurize it or drink it, but people who do these things are not called MILKMAN. And other pairs of bases where the head is MAN don't necessarily carry meanings to do with delivery: POSTMAN does, but DUSTMAN has a meaning opposite to delivery. In TAXMAN the two elements are related in quite a different way, as they are in DOORMAN.

5.2 Here are some compound nouns with a structure in common. What is that structure, i.e. to what lexical categories do the two bases

EXERCISES ✎

belong? Can you say anything about the meaning of the structure as such, and about head–dependent relations (see **Unit 4**)?

matchbox	tombstone	trouser-press
facecloth	cat-basket	broom cupboard
bedroom	football stadium	address-book
cash-crop	leg-room	flower vase
hairbrush		

5.3 What do the structures of the following compounds mean? Note carefully where one member of the compound has an internal structure of its own. Think of three words of a similar structure having a similar general meaning to each of them.

death-defying	town planning	rocking chair
show-stopper	boyfriend	churchgoer

Discussion

Some of these look similar to each other, on the face of it. DEATH-DEFYING and TOWN PLANNING appear to be both [noun + verb in -ING]. But DEATH-DEFYING is an adjective and TOWN PLANNING is a noun, in their most typical uses. In any case, PLANNING is really a noun here. SHOW-STOPPER and CHURCH-GOER are both of the structure [noun + noun in *-er*] but they have different meanings, CHURCHGOER being related to GO TO CHURCH, where *to church* indicates direction to place, whereas SHOW-STOPPER is related to STOP THE SHOW, where THE SHOW is simply the (direct) object of *stop*. (If you don't know this grammatical terminology, see David Crystal's book *Rediscover Grammar* (Longman, 1988).)

Other multi-part bases are structured in more complicated ways. They have a central element or root to which affixes are attached, and those affixes – BOUND DERIVATIONAL MORPHEMES or LEXICAL AFFIXES – don't express grammatical meaning but have as their main job the formation of a lexeme with a different sense or senses from the root itself, as we saw in **Unit 3**:

Bound derivational morphemes
Lexical affixes

fail-ure	confess-or	group-ie	pack-age	post-al
sub-human	para-medic	be-fuddle	de-select	tri-cycle

The first row has words consisting of a root followed by an affix, and the second row a root preceded by an affix. In each instance, grammatical affixes must be added to the complete stem and not to the component parts (*confessors, paramedics*, not *confessesors, *parasmedics*), just as you would expect from our discussion in **Units 2–4** (especially Exercise 3.3). Lexemes of this type, with bases consisting of a root and affixes, are called COMPLEX, and have complex bases.

Complex lexemes

5.4 Which of the following lexemes are compound and which are complex? Say which elements are affixes (if any).

EXERCISES

postbox *d*	pre-war *x*	pro-life *x*	weekly *x*
strongly *x*	stomach-ache *d*	tone-poem *d*	oddity *x*
weakness *x*	schmaltzy *x*	illicit *x*	lifestyle *d*
brake fluid *d*	Calvinism *x*	grammarian *x*	minicab *d*
unquiet *x*	homeless *x*	womanhood *d*	hereby *d*

That exercise was quite easy. You've done similar things several times already in this book. But it becomes much more interesting when we ask what the *job* is of any particular affix in a complex base. A typical good answer will include two sorts of information:

Discussion

(i) it makes an A into a B (where A and B are lexical categories, and where in some instances A and B may be the same) For instance, in the case of HOMELESS, the affix -LESS has the job of making a noun (HOME) into an adjective.

(ii) the B that it makes has a particular sort of meaning

Again with HOMELESS, we note that the particular job of -LESS is to make an adjective with the meaning 'not having (an) X', where X is the root. Most importantly, we have RECURRENCE (see **Unit 1**); this isn't just a property of the word HOMELESS, but of significant numbers of words with the same structure:

heartless	strapless
breathless	spotless
useless	priceless
treeless	friendless
endless	powerless

In some of these instances you may have to work a bit at the meaning – for instance HEARTLESS is normally used only metaphorically ('not having a heart' = 'mean, uncharitable') and SPOTLESS is normally applied only in a particular sense of SPOT, namely 'dirty mark' (and also metaphorically, 'not having a dirty mark' = 'irreproachable (as of a reputation)'). But with these reservations, you will notice that words structured in this way have meanings which are predictable from their shapes and from the meanings of their parts.

Try the kind of exercise involving the words in -LESS, but this time with some different affixes of English.

5.5 What do the following make into what? (Can that question always be answered?) What is the particular sort of meaning which the resulting lexical word has?

inter-   -age
-ly   mono-
-est   -ant/-ent (treat as if the same)
arch-   -er/-or (treat as if the same)
-ous

5.6 Some of these have more than one function. Which?

5.7 Are there any significant differences between the behaviour of affixes before and after the root, to judge by the data above?

5.8 My daughter invented the lexeme BLONDENER. Explain its structure and work out its meaning.

Recap discussion

Some of the affixes appear to have a different sort of job, that is, not signalling the lexical category of the resulting word, but carrying some kind of lexical meaning which is put together with that of what precedes or follows to build the lexical meaning of the resultant word. They are examples of BOUND LEXICAL MORPHEMES (see **Unit 3**). MONO- is one of those. It just means 'one' – so for example MONOLINGUAL (*mono-lingu-al*) means what it does according to the structure 'one + language + adjective-affix', i.e. 'having the property of (using just) one language'. MONOCULTURE (*mono-culture*) means 'one + culture (in the sense of 'crop')' and MONOTHEISM (*mono-the-ism*) means 'one + god + system-of-belief'.

The lexeme MONOTHEISM also shows that -ISM is partially an example of the same phenomenon. The affix has the meaning 'system of belief', but also indicates the fact that the word is a noun.

5.9 Make a list of six other elements like this which behave like MONO-. (*Hint*: scientific terminology is an especially good place to find them. Think about, for example, TELE-, -IDE, -GEN, or -ASE, and expand the list.)

You may not with absolute confidence be able to decide in every case whether these are true affixes or bound morphemes serving as lexical elements. If they are the former, the resultant structures are complex; if the latter, they are compound.

5.10 What are the jobs of the following affixes in English? Remember the two sorts of answer that are required (see page 37), and try to think of at least six words with the same structure to check that there is really something in common between them.

conserv-ATION	paint-ER	afford-ABLE
music-AL	UN-dress	criminal-IZE
brew-ERY	humid-ITY	RE-visit
escap-IST	bold-NESS	HYPER-active
PRE-pack-AGE	(a) paint-ING	UN-happy
Thatcher-ITE	DIS-member	green-ISH
NON-stop		

Discussion

Whilst you are thinking of examples, you may come across some that don't fit the pattern at all. Where this happens, we need to say that there may be absolute exceptions to a pattern. How many words can you think of that are structured in the same way as FORGIVENESS, for instance – a verb with an affix *-ness* that makes it a noun? Or FASHIONABLE – an adjective with the affix *-able* that appears to be built on a noun, and with an unpredictable meaning, 'in line with the current taste of influential people'? (Note that there could be a regular FASHIONABLE, as in *Sculptures are fashionable out of mashed potato* – 'able to be fashioned', with the verb FASHION parallel to the AFFORD in AFFORDABLE – 'able to be afforded'.)

You'll almost certainly think of some sets of words that seem to suggest a different pattern from the one suggested by the word I've given. I've indicated a possibility for you to consider by putting two UN- words in the above exercise. When this happens, you should consider that you are dealing with two different elements that just happen to be written or pronounced identically.

OUTCOMES OF UNIT 5

Skills learnt

- associating patterns with meanings
- discriminating different sorts of compound
- discriminating compounds from complexes
- finding further examples of a pattern from your own vocabulary

Terms learnt

COMPOUND; COMPLEX; LEXICAL AFFIX (BOUND DERIVATIONAL MORPHEME)

Principles learnt

- Compounds do not show a consistent meaning-relation between their bases, but there are some patterns which can be related to sentence-meanings.
- Complexes often show more consistent meaning patterns.

Topics further practised

- identifying lexical and grammatical morphemes

6 IDENTIFYING GRAMMATICAL MORPHEMES

> Identifying grammatical morphemes in Turkish and Latin, and modifying your analysis as new data becomes available. How grammatical information can be expressed in affixes. Oddities in paradigms.

Languages vary in the ease with which individual items of grammatical information can be recovered from their word-structure. Turkish has very transparent word structure, Latin less so. We'll work through some data from both these languages in a special kind of extended exercise. You'll be asked to make statements about the structure of the words presented, and modify your ideas in the light of further data. This mirrors the linguist's professional activity, or in fact any scientific activity: forming hypotheses on the basis of the data available, then modifying them in the light of further data.

TURKISH

In this exercise you will be invited to modify your analysis as you go along. It may be distracting if you already know some Turkish.

EXERCISES ✎

6.1 Identify which morphemes mean what in the following verb-forms:

geliyorum	I am coming (1)
geliyoruz	we are coming (1)
geliyorsun	you (SG) are coming (2)
geliyorsunuz	you (PL) are coming (2)
geliyor	he/she is coming (3)
geliyorlar	they are coming (3)

Notions such as 'I', 'you', 'we', 'they' represent the grammatical cate-gory of PERSON, conventionally called *1st*, *2nd* and *3rd* as indicated by the figures in brackets. Each of these forms exhibits NUMBER, either singular or plural. (Don't confuse that with the 'number' in brackets, which relates to person.) In future Exercises, data will be presented in diagrams (matrices, PARADIGMS) organized according to notions like these. There is also grammatical information here about TENSE or time-reference, but we can ignore that temporarily.

6.2 On the basis of what you have seen, and of adding the following data, what is the stem meaning 'come' and what means:

I	?
you (sing.)	?
he/she (not distinguished in Turkish)	?
we	?
you (pl.)	?
they	?

6.3 (a) On the basis of the data below, what means 'past tense, continuous aspect (= English BE + -ING)' in Turkish?
    (b) What, on the basis of *all* the data presented so far in this Unit, is the Turkish for 'you (singular)' in verb forms?

number	SG	PL
person		
1	*geliyordum*	*geliyorduk*
2	*geliyordun*	*geliyordunuz*
3	*geliyordu*	*geliyordular*

These forms mean 'I was coming', etc.

Discussion

It is neatest to analyse *-du-* in the same way in each form, i.e. in each form as 'past tense, continuous aspect'; which leaves *-n* in the meaning 'you (singular)'. If that is the form that appears in the first data-set, then we have a form *-su-* there left over to assign a meaning to. '2nd person (= 'you') and present tense' seems a good idea, i.e. both meanings folded into one form. In this way, we extract the maximum amount of consistent patterning out of our data; *-du-* always means the same and 'past continuous' is always expressed in the same way. We could say that *-um* always means '1st person, continuous aspect' in the two data-sets; but that would mean we would have to segment *geliyordum* as *geliyor-d-um* and we would have a blip: 'past continuous' would sometimes be *-du-* and some-times *-d-*.

Another analytic style is to identify the two relevant morphemes in *geliyordum* as *-du-* and *-um*, and to say that there is a kind of

tidying-up rule of spelling and/or pronunciation which deletes one
-*u*- before another -*u*-. This style of analysis has many adherents. Its
advantage here is that it enables us to maintain the analysis that
-*du*- and -*um*, in the particular meanings mentioned here, always have
the same shape. The cost is an ABSTRACT ANALYSIS suggesting that
geliyordum is 'really' *geliyorduum; if you're literal-minded, it implies
that bits of pronunciation go unheard.

Abstract analysis

6.4 On the basis of the following data, what is the morpheme
meaning 'not'? Using data from previous exercises also, predict the
Turkish for 'you (plural) were not coming'.

number	SG	PL
person		
1	*gelmiyorum* 'I am not coming' [etc.]	*gelmiyoruz*
2	*gelmiyorsun*	*gelmiyorsunuz*
3	*gelmiyor*	*gelmiyorlar*

6.5 On the basis of the following data, what is the morpheme
meaning 'shall/will' (= future tense)?

6.6 How do you form the future stem in Turkish?
  (The data has been slightly simplified.)

number	SG	PL
person		
1	*gelecekim* 'I shall come' [etc.]	*gelecekiz*
2	*geleceksin*	*geleceksiniz*
3	*gelecek*	*gelecekler*

6.7 On the basis of the following data, what is the morpheme
meaning 'habitually' (= habitual aspect)? How do you form the
habitual stem?

number	SG	PL
person		
1	*gelirim* 'I habitually come' [etc.]	*geliriz*
2	*gelirsin*	*gelirsiniz*
3	*gelir*	*gelirler*

6.8 Reconsider your earlier identification of the stem meaning
'come'. Can you say what -*iyor*- might mean?

6.9 Predict the Turkish forms for 'I habitually came', 'you (singular) habitually came' and so on.

You will probably make a couple of mistakes, but don't worry – you could not have avoided doing so on the data presented here. You can come up with an intelligent analysis that's wrong. This will be explained!

6.10 What relation can you see amongst the various personal affixes? How consistent is Turkish in expressing the same information about (1st/2nd/3rd) person?

Here is some data that corresponds to some of the Turkish material just given. **LATIN**

6.11 On the basis of the following data, what is the stem of the verb meaning 'to come' in Latin and what means:

I	?
you (sing.)	?
he/she (not distinguished in Latin)	?
we	?
you (pl.)	?
they	?

number	SG	PL
person		
1	venio 'I am coming' [etc.]	venimus
2	venis	venitis
3	venit	veniunt

6.12 On the basis of the following data, what means 'past tense, continuous aspect' (= English BE + -ING), traditionally called 'imperfect'?

6.13 Does the analysis you made of the personal affixes (corresponding to 'I', 'you', etc.) change as a result of adding this new data?

number	SG	PL
person		
1	veniebam 'I was coming' [etc.]	veniebamus
2	veniebas	veniebatis
3	veniebat	veniebant

6.14   What, on the basis of all the data so far, is the Latin for 'you (singular)' in verb forms?

6.15   What needs to be changed in your analysis so far of person and number marking to accommodate the following new data for the past tense (traditionally called 'perfect')?

number	SG	PL
person		
1	*veni* 'I came' [etc.]	*venimus*
2	*venisti*	*venistis*
3	*venit*	*venerunt*

Review what you have decided so far about the Latin morpheme meaning 'past tense, continuous aspect (= BE + -ING, traditionally called 'imperfect')'. Then consider this new data:

rogare 'to ask'	*rogo* 'I ask'	*rogabam* 'I was asking'
festinare 'to hurry'	*festino* 'I hurry'	*festinabam* 'I was hurrying'
celare 'to hide'	*celo* 'I hide'	*celabam* 'I was hiding'
placere 'to please'	*placeo* 'I please'	*placebam* 'I was pleasing'
suadere 'to advise'	*suadeo* 'I advise'	*suadebam* 'I was advising'
audere 'to dare'	*audeo* 'I dare'	*audebam* 'I was (being) daring'
ducere 'to lead'	*duco* 'I lead'	*ducebam* 'I was leading'
mittere 'to send'	*mitto* 'I send'	*mittebam* 'I was sending'
tangere 'to touch'	*tango* 'I touch'	*tangebam* 'I was touching'
iacere 'to throw'	*iacio* 'I throw'	*iaciebam* 'I was throwing'
facere 'to make'	*facio* 'I make'	*faciebam* 'I was making'
quatere 'to shake'	*quatio* 'I shake'	*quatiebam* 'I was shaking'
farcire 'to stuff'	*farcio* 'I stuff'	*farciebam* 'I was stuffing'
sepelire 'to bury'	*sepelio* 'I bury'	*sepeliebam* 'I was burying'

EXERCISES ✎

6.16   In the light of this material, what do you now consider the imperfect morpheme described above to be? Say exactly how you have changed your previous analysis.

6.17   Identify the stems of the verbs in the last set of data, stating what difficulties you had in doing this, if any.

6.18   On the evidence of this set, what is the Latin for '1st person, singular number (= 'I')'? Again, state the difficulties in making your decision, if any.

6.19 We have seen instances where more than one meaning – i.e. grammatical meaning – is packed into one single morpheme. Look back over your Turkish and Latin analyses and find one in each language.

This is entirely normal in the world's languages, and can be identified in English also.

6.20 What is meant by the affix in examples of English verbs such as the following?

> speak-s   sweat-s   wash-es

We can say that *-(e)s* is the CUMULATIVE expression of all these meanings at once.

Important: notice that if you were analysing *sweated (sweat-ed)*, you'd say that the *-ed* just marked tense (past). Why not person and number as well – *I sweated*, *we sweated*, *they sweated*? Well, there are no actual distinctions of person and number marked in the past tense at all; in principle, you could say either that *-ed* marked all three persons and both numbers, or that it doesn't mark person and number at all. The second way of putting it is far more economical, and also more sensible; you just don't refer to any distinctions that aren't marked. So *-ed* expresses only tense (past); we can say that it is DIRECT expression of that grammatical meaning.

Discussion
Cumulative

Direct

Below are listed some Russian verb-forms and noun-forms, arranged in paradigms. (*Note*: gender is ignored.)

RUSSIAN

6.21 Which affixes are direct (express a single grammatical meaning), and which ones are cumulative (express more than one grammatical meaning at once)?

EXERCISES ✎

Verb: DUMAT′ 'to think'

ASPECT: Imperfective

Aspect

Tense person/ number	non-past	past	Tense person/ number	non-past	past
1 SG	*dumaju*	*dumal*	1 PL	*dumaem*	*dumali*
2 SG	*dumaeʃ′*	*dumal*	2 PL	*dumaete*	*dumali*
3 SG	*dumaet*	*dumal*	3 PL	*dumajut*	*dumali*

Aspect: Perfective

Tense person/ number	non-past	past	Tense person/ number	non-past	past
1 SG	*podumaju*	*podumal*	1 PL	*podumaem*	*podumali*
2 SG	*podumaeʃ'*	*podumal*	2 PL	*podumaete*	*podumali*
3 SG	*podumaet*	*podumal*	3 PL	*podumajut*	*podumali*

Noun: SLOVO 'word'

number case	singular	plural
Accusative	*slovo*	*slova*
Genitive	*slova*	*slov*
Dative	*slovu*	*slovam*
Instrumental	*slovom*	*slovami*
Prepositional	*slove*	*slovax*

Treat the two forms *slova* as being just coincidentally the same – i.e. there is no hidden significance in their sameness. (In fact, they have different stress patterns, and are thus not really identical at all. But I am ignoring the complications of stress in this exercise.)

OUTCOMES OF UNIT 6

Skills learnt

- prediction of forms on the basis of already-known data
- explicit formulation of problems arising in the course of analysis
- modification of analyses in the light of further data
- perceiving simple and complex relations between grammatical features and grammatical morphemes

Terms learnt

ABSTRACT ANALYSIS; CUMULATIVE; DIRECT

Principles learnt

- Generalizations should be expressed in such a way as to cover the maximum number of cases, and 'bigger' generalizations take precedence.
- The same data may be analysed in different ways, according to analytic style.

Topics further practised

- segmentation and classification

WHERE TO FIX AFFIXES

7

> The different positions that affixes may occupy within the word. An alternative to affixation.

In **Unit 4**, we noted that bases could be associated with one or more additional bound elements hanging round the edge of them. These extra elements are called AFFIXES, and they serve a number of different functions, both lexical and grammatical.

Affixes are classified structurally by the positions they can occupy, so let's look at the full range of positions that it is possible for them to occupy. In each instance, I'll illustrate using only grammatical affixes whose position is defined in relation to a stem.

1. SUFFIXES (sometimes called *postfixes*): the affixed morpheme goes after the stem.

SUFFIXES

Suffixes

In Russian the noun GAZETA 'newspaper' comes in the word-forms *gazeta, gazetu, gazety, gazete, gazetoj, gazet, gazetam, gazetami, gazetax*. They are distributed according to the paradigm below. You don't need to know what the names of the cases mean; the only important thing is that they have different grammatical meanings.

number	singular	plural
case		
Nominative	*gazeta*	*gazety*
Accusative	*gazetu*	*gazety*
Genitive	*gazety*	*gazet*
Dative	*gazete*	*gazetam*
Instrumental	*gazetoj*	*gazetami*
Prepositional	*gazete*	*gazetax*

EXERCISE ✎

7.1 Recap question: Can you separate the information about case from the information about number in these forms?

We can regard *gazet-*, which is common to all these forms, as the stem, and the rest as affixed markers of number and case. One form is unaffixed, of course – did you spot it (it means 'of newspapers')?

In Yidiny, a Pama-Nyungan language of Australia, the verb WAWA 'to see' comes in the following forms:

wawa
wawal
wawalnyu
wawalna
wawalji

These differences partly encode time-reference (e.g. past vs. future) and partly other meanings such as 'fear lest what the verb denotes should happen' (something like 'for God's sake don't let me ever have to see . . .') or 'do what the verb denotes for some particular named purpose'. *Wawa* is the stem here, and *-l-* a special meaning-less affix (called an AUGMENT) added to all forms of this verb except the form for giving commands *wawa* ('see!'). The morphs after the augment *-l-* are also affixes, of course.

Augment

In spoken Welsh the verb AGOR ('to open') comes in the following forms, all of which denote past time:

number	SG	PL
person		
1	*agores*	*agoron*
2	*agorest*	*agoroch*
3	*agorodd*	*agoron*

EXERCISE ✎

7.2 What is the stem of these forms above?

The differences in the affixes are due to the person of the subject (i.e. respectively whether I, you (singular), he or she, we or they, or you (plural) performed the opening).

PREFIXES

Prefixes

2. PREFIXES: the affixed morpheme goes before the stem.

In Swahili, a major official language in the Bantu sub-family of the Niger-Congo family spoken in East Africa, verbs are constructed with their subject, tense-marker (time-reference marker) and object before the stem, strictly in that order, as in *nitawapenda*: *-penda* may be taken as the stem of the lexeme meaning 'to like', and *ni-* is 'I', *ta-* 'future' and *wa-* 'them', and the whole means 'I will like them'. Thus also *a-li-ku-penda* = 's/he-past-you-like' = 's/he liked you'. Each morpheme before the stem is a prefix. All three available positions can be filled with a prefix, the first two obligatorily, yielding a structure like this:

> subject   tense   direct object   stem

In Chamorro, an Austronesian language of Guam island, verbs form their corresponding verbal noun by a special kind of prefixing rule.

7.3 How exactly are such verbal nouns made? (Note that *'* is a consonant, and an acute accent marks the stressed syllable.)

EXERCISE ✎

	verb	derived verbal noun
'look at'	atan	á'atan
'see'	li'e'	líli'e'
'lift'	hatsa	háhatsa
'fish'	peska	pépeska
'fall'	poddong	pópoddong
'stay, live'	saga	sásaga

This particular sort of prefixing process is called REDUPLICATION.

Discussion
Reduplication

3. INFIXES: the affixed morpheme is placed within the stem.

INFIXES

Infixes

This is characteristic of some Philippine languages; in Bontok, a Malayo-Polynesian language of the Philippines, a marker *-um-* meaning something like 'is becoming' or 'future', can be placed within a stem (of any lexical category), for example:

bato	'stone'	bumato	'is turning to stone'
pusi	'poor'	pumusi	'is becoming poor'
kilad	'red'	kumilad	'is becoming red'
sulat	'read'	sumulat	'is starting to read'
tengao	'have a holiday'	tumengao-	'will have a holiday'

7.4 How can you describe precisely where to put the marker?

EXERCISE ✎

A special type of infixation can be seen in Arabic, whereby the consonants of a stem carry the lexical (dictionary) meaning whilst the vowels between them may in some instances carry grammatical meaning. In Egyptian Arabic, for instance, two ways of expressing the difference between singular and plural in nouns are as follows:

(1)

sign	'prison'	*suguun*	'prisons'
farq	'difference'	*furuuq*	'differences'
dars	'lesson'	*duruus*	'lessons'
xadd	'cheek'	*xuduud*	'cheeks'
raff	'shelf'	*rufuuf*	'shelves'

(2)

maʕmal	'laboratory'	*maʕaamil*	'laboratories'
maʕlaqa	'spoon'	*maʕaaliq*	'spoons'
markib	'ship'	*maraakib*	'ships'
gardal	'bucket'	*garaadil*	'buckets'

Not all the singulars in each data-set are parallel in construction, but the plurals are.

EXERCISES ✎   **7.5**   Describe the two plural patterns in terms of their vowel and consonant structure. (The letter ʕ represents a consonant sound.)

7.6   What is the plural form of the following Arabic words? The first three are in group (1) and the second three in group (2).

qaṣr	'palace'
bank	'bank'
fann	'skill, technique'
zawba'a	'storm'
kanyisa	'church'
madrasa	'school'

True infixation is absent in English. Here is an instance from Latin, with minor adjustment to the spelling in one instance to make the point clearer.

1 SG present	1 SG preterite	Supine	
Name of form:			
rumpo	*rupi*	*ruptum*	'break apart'
frango	*fregi*	*fragtum*	'break'
(*in*)*cumbo*	(*in*)*cubui*	(*in*)*cubitum*	'lie (on)'
–	*liqui*	*lictum*	'leave'

Here we have roots *rup-*, *frag-* and *cub-*, into which an *-m-* or an *-n-* (depending on which consonant sound follows) has been inserted to make the base which is the present stem. *cub-* is found in a few words of English, borrowed from Latin; *cumb-* is found in a few others.

7.7 Note the meaning of *cu(m)b-* in Latin, and see whether you can identify any of these borrowings. Can you work out what the missing form of the verb meaning 'leave' is, based on the pattern and on your knowledge of English words derived from it?

EXERCISE ✎

---

4.   CIRCUMFIXES: the affix is placed around the stem

One way of analysing the past participle of German verbs, such as *gebrochen* ('broken'), *gesungen*, ('sung'), *geöffnet* ('opened'), *geschneit* ('snowed'), is to say that the special past participle marker consists of both a prefix (*ge-*) and a suffix (*-en* or *-(e)t*), which may be thought of as a single element or morpheme surrounding the stem: a circumfix. In some German verbs, the second part alone is used, for example *verrechn-et* ('miscalculated').

CIRCUMFIXES

Circumfixes

Now some practice in identifying affixes and attempting to assign a meaning to them.

Nahuatl is an Uto-Aztecan language spoken in Mexico, whose classical form was the administrative language of the Aztec empire in the sixteenth century.

NAHUATL

Below are listed some forms of the Classical Nahuatl verb 'to cry', given mainly in traditional Aztec spelling except that a colon indicating vowel length has been introduced.

nicho:ca	'I cry'
nicho:cani	'I am crying'
cho:cani	's/he is crying'
ticho:cas	'you (singular) will cry'
nicho:cas	'I will cry'
cho:cayah	'they were crying'
ancho:cah	'you (plural) cry'
ticho:cayah	'we were crying'
cho:ca	's/he cries'
ancho:cayah	'you (plural) were crying'
ticho:canih	'we are crying'
cho:canih	'they are crying'
cho:cah	'they cry'
ticho:canih	'we are crying'

Start by organizing the data into a PARADIGM (see **Unit 2**), i.e. make a table or matrix of cells showing what meanings are encoded and place the forms into those cells. You'll need PERSON (1st, 2nd, 3rd), NUMBER (singular or plural), TENSE (past, present or future) and ASPECT (here progressive or non-progressive, as represented in English by 'I am crying' vs. 'I cry'). I suggest you make a grid of person and number for each separate combination of tense and aspect (e.g. present progressive). You won't find a future progressive ('will be crying') or a past non-progressive ('cried'). Some cells, of course, will be empty; you'll soon be asked to fill them in.

EXERCISES 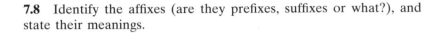 7.8 Identify the affixes (are they prefixes, suffixes or what?), and state their meanings.

7.9 What is Nahuatl for the following meanings, whose cells will be empty in your paradigm?

'you (singular) are crying'	?
'I was crying'	?
'she will cry'	?
'you (plural) will cry'	?

7.10 Here is some further Classical Nahuatl data. State the affixal ways in which the plural of animate nouns may be formed.

ti:ci-tl	'midwife'	*ti:ti:cih*	'midwives'
coyo:-tl	'coyote'	*co:coyoh*	'coyotes'
teo:-tl	'god'	*te:teoh*	'gods'
tepe:tl	'mountain'	*te:tepeh*	'mountains'
co:a:tl	'snake'	*co:co:ah*	'snakes'
te:uc-tli	'lord'	*te:te:uctin*	'lords'
pil-li	'nobleman'	*pi:piltin*	'noblemen'
cih-tli	'hare'	*ci:cihtin*	'hares'
ichca-tl	'sheep'	*i:ichcameh*	'sheep'
wi:lo:tl	'dove'	*wi:wi:lomeh*	'doves'

Discussion Firstly, notice that the suffix needs to be discarded to arrive at the form of the stem. One of the suffixes -*h*, -*tin* or -*meh* is added, depending on which noun is in question, to the stem to form the plural. With the first and third of these, any long vowel right at the end of the stem is shortened. In addition, the first consonant (if there is one) and vowel of the stem are used as a reduplicative prefix, with the vowel always pronounced long irrespective of its length in the stem of the singular.

7.11 What might the plural of *oce:lo:-tl* ('jaguar') and -*po:ch-tli* ('young man') be?

Fula (Fulani, Fulfulde) is a western Niger-Congo language spoken in various places in inland sub-Saharan West Africa.

Verb-forms in Fula may contain a so-called intensive root-extender, meaning roughly 'very much', as shown below:

fooDa	'pull'	*fooDta*	'pull very tight', etc
saDa	'be difficult'	*saDta*	
nyaaDa	'be bitter'	*nyaaDta*	
leesa	'be low'	*leest*	
yana	'fall'	*yanta*	'fall heavily'
majja	'get lost'	*majjita*	
yaaja	'be wide'	*yaajita*	
daro	'stand'	*darto*	'stand firm'
salo	'refuse'	*salto*	'refuse point-blank'
taBo	'catch'	*taBto*	'catch firmly'
kaaso	'fall short'	*kaasto*	
heesho	'be older'	*Badto*	

7.12 How many different shapes does the intensive morpheme show up in?

7.13 How is the intensive form of verbs made?

Koryak is a language of the Palaeo-Siberian (Chukchi-Kamchatkan) group, spoken in the far east of Russia.

Examine the following forms, the paradigm of the verb 'begin', and answer the questions.

Theoretical form of the stem: *ŋəvok*

tense	present	past	future
person/number			
1 SG	təŋvotkən	təŋvok	tətaŋvoŋ
2 SG	ŋəvotkən	ŋəvojja	taŋvoŋə
3 SG	ŋəvotkən	ŋəvojja	taŋvoŋə
1 PL	mətəŋvolatkən	mətəŋvolamək	məttaŋvolamək
2 PL	ŋəvolatkənetək	ŋəvolatək	taŋvolatək
3 PL	ŋəvolatkən	ŋəvolat	taŋvolaŋ

7.14 What sort of an affix is *la*? What does it mean?

7.15 What sort of an affix is *tə*? What does it mean?

7.16 What means 'present tense'?

(There is far more to this data than is explored by the questions.)

GERMAN

Circumfixation in German was mentioned above. Here are some German verbs with their structure shown by means of hyphenation.

EXERCISE ✎

7.17 What determines whether the circumfix *ge ... -(e)t* or *-en* is used, and what determines whether *-(e)t* or *-en* alone is used to form the perfective participle? (Don't worry about why *-(e)t* rather than *-en* might be chosen – that's not the point of this exercise.)

infinitive	past participle	
be-komm-en	*be-komm-en*	'get'
sag-en	*ge-sag-t*	'say'
schreib-en	*ge-schrieb-en*	'write'
hinter-geh-en	*hinter-gang-en*	'deceive'
ver-säum-en	*ver-säum-t*	'delay'
durch-bohr-en	*durch-bohr-t*	'perforate'
zeichn-en	*ge-zeichn-et*	'draw'
wieder-hol-en	*wieder-hol-t*	'repeat'
hab-en	*ge-hab-t*	' have'
sing-en	*ge-sung-en*	'sing'
acht-en	*ge-acht-et*	'heed'
ver-acht-en	*ver-acht-et*	'despise'

In the left column, in each instance, *-en* is added to the verb stem to make the infinitive form; this is disregarded when constructing the participle form.

There are also methods of signalling grammatical differences which don't involve affixation of any kind, but which are also not CONVERSIONS such as we saw at the end of **Unit 4**. One is illustrated by English *ring*, *rang* and *rung* as grammatical word-forms of TO RING; this method of forming grammatical words is called by the German

Ablaut

technical term ABLAUT. The differences in vowel choice signal differences of grammatical meaning, but the pattern is not widespread enough in English for us to be able to say that, for instance, *-a-* means 'past tense'. That would be true for only a handful of verbs like TO RUN, TO COME, TO SING, TO SINK – and even then not for all speakers of English, as we'll see later. Worse still, the *-a-* is not pronounced the same in all four of the verbs mentioned. The Arabic instances cited in the data for Exercise 7.5 above clearly show some affinity with ablaut as well as with infixation; the vowel patterns there signal grammatical information.

7.18   Why aren't the English forms mentioned examples of conversion?

7.19   How would you classify the way of forming the plural of the following nouns in Maori, the indigenous Malayo-Polynesian language of New Zealand?

	SG	PL
'woman'	*wahine*	*waahine*
'parent'	*matua*	*maatua*
'ancestor'	*tipuna*	*tiipuna*

OUTCOMES OF UNIT 7

- distinguishing partly similar affixation-types

Skills learnt

AFFIX; PREFIX; REDUPLICATION; SUFFIX; INFIX; CIRCUMFIX; ABLAUT; AUGMENT

Terms learnt

- Information expressible by affixation can be represented by other word-formational methods.

Principles learnt

- paradigm construction and prediction of unknown word-forms

Topics further practised

8 WORD-FORMATION BY REDUCTION

> Numerous different methods of abbreviation.

So far we have looked at methods of word-formation involving extension of bases by the addition of morphemes (AFFIXATION) and change of shape without the use of additional elements (ABLAUT and some instances of CONVERSION). Language-users also have at their disposal a range of devices whose effect is to shorten words or longer lexical expressions, i.e. ABBREVIATIONS. The consequence of this, of course, is to disfigure or even kill off any morphological structure in those expressions.

EXERCISES **8.1** What are the following expressions typically reduced to?

girocheque
violoncello
personal identification
    number
identity card
facsimile

European currency unit
bovine spongiform
    encephalopathy
vegetarian (or vegetable)
    hamburger

Discussion ECU is of some interest, as it is identical to an ancient French coin-name meaning 'shield'. This will obviously ease the new word's passage into French, but may stiffen the resistance of English-users.

8.2 In the last example in the above exercise, notice that a reduction probably took place in the second word before it ever got into the same expression as VEGETARIAN. What reduction?

Sometimes the shortened expressions achieve the status of the normal expression for what is meant, and the older, longer forms disappear. In addition to some in the list above, a good example is PRAM, which has pushed out PERAMBULATOR, the word from which it originates, pretty well completely. In other cases, the longer version was only ever in use among specialists, and the shortened version is the only one ever known among ordinary people. One of these is LASER, once LIGHT AMPLIFICATION BY STIMU-LATED EMISSION OF RADIATION, and another is AIDS, from ACQUIRED IMMUNE DEFICIENCY SYNDROME. How wide-spread the longer usage ever was, even among specialists, is not clear in every instance. HYPE is clearly short for something begin-ning with HYPER-, but it isn't obvious what (any ideas?). Sometimes it is clear that a longer form has been invented to 'explain' a snappy shorter word that the inventors wish to use come hell or high water. This is particularly noticeable in the names of political pressure groups; as for instance *Action on Smoking and Health*, better known as ASH, with its obvious pun. Most often, such abbreviations arise from the written form of expressions rather than the spoken form. Clipping does not pay any systematic attention to the morphology of the expressions being clipped.

Many words have been formed, and are still regularly formed, by these processes. Clipping the ends of words is called by linguists APOCOPE; it is seen in TELLY (with minor respelling), SLO-MO (two words here undergoing the same process – in spelling, at least), SITCOM (two words again), E-MAIL or EMAIL. What are the orig-inal words which have suffered clipping in these examples?

A particularly spectacular instance is TAXI, clipped by apocope from TAXI-CAB. Each of these elements is itself the result of clipping by apocope, TAXI from TAXIMETER and CAB from CABRIOLET.

Clipping of beginnings, or PROCOPE, is seen in BUS (now universal, though originally from OMNIBUS) and the -ZINE (from MAGA-ZINE) used in FANZINE 'magazine for fans (of a team, a band, etc.)'.

SIMPLE ABBREVIATION: CLIPPING BEGINNINGS OR ENDS

Apocope

Procope

8.3 What is the origin of FAN, in FANZINE?

EXERCISE ✎

Clipping of both ends, often but not always just leaving the stressed syllable of the word, is seen in FLU (from INFLUENZA) and TEC (from DETECTIVE); this used to be widespread in slang but it has passed its sell-by date a bit.

The result of clipping may sometimes be a new affix with the characteristics of a bound lexical morpheme (see **Unit 4**). One of these may be HOMO-, a clipped form of HOMOSEXUAL and used in the same sense as a separate element in HOMOPHOBIA (it happens to coincide with the HOMO- out of which HOMOSEXUAL was originally coined, a bound lexical morpheme meaning 'same'). An older instance is MINI- from MINIATURE or MINIMUM or both.

EXERCISE ✎

8.4 Below are some clipped words, some of them extended by suffixation. The list includes some clippings reused in still other words. What is the original word or expression? Can you say exactly what process or processes have been involved in the creation of each?

fridge	cyborg	Becky	coke
movie	electrocute	europhile	cami-knickers
Spurs	Lambo	loony	(a bunch of) mums
Gers	Oz	rugger	Tanzania
con-man	detox	Mountie	alco-pop
cute	dis	Herts	

BLENDS

Blending occurs when two words are amalgamated to form a single one, usually by simply placing together the first part of one and the last part of another, irrespective of any morpheme boundaries in the bases. Two very familiar blends are SMOG, from SMOKE + FOG, and BRUNCH, from BREAKFAST + LUNCH. The result is a word whose meaning is relevant to the meaning of both of the source words. A weaker form of blending is when one word is imported whole into the reduced frame of the other, as in SKYJACK, with SKY inserted into a reduced HIJACK.

EXERCISE ✎

8.5 What words have been blended in the creation of the following? Which represent the weaker form of blending and which the stronger?

breathalyser   paratrooper

motel   chunnel

transistor   travelator

guesstimate

TELESCOPING

Telescoping is a type of blending where two (or possibly more) words are formed into one by the omission of a portion of one word duplicated in the other, as in GLITTERATI ('successful intellectuals in the arts') from GLITTER and LITTERATI; SLANGUAGE you can work out for yourself.

8.6 If you consider the pronunciation, rather than the spelling, one of the words in the above Exercise 8.5 turns out to be of this type; which?

EXERCISE ✎

An acronym in the restricted sense is a word formed by the initial letters of the words of a longer expression, pronounceable as a natural word of the language in question. LASER, explained above, is one of these, and SNAFU is another (from SITUATION NORMAL, ALL FOULED UP; or, according to some, ALL FUCKED UP). WYSIWYG is another – where does it come from? The term acronym may be used in an extended sense to cover initialisms.

ACRONYMY

Initialisms are words formed from the initial letters which continue to be pronounced as a string of letters, whether or not that string could represent a pronounceable word. Current English examples include E, K, uPVC, CFC, PDQ, PC (in two senses), CD and OTT. In some cases, the origin will be known to most users of the language (CD, PDQ, OTT), in others perhaps not so widely, especially if the source expression is the scientific name of a synthetic chemical (uPVC, CFC), for instance.

INITIALISM

8.7 Are the following acronyms (in the restricted sense) or initialisms? Not everyone will come to the same conclusion about every instance.

EXERCISES ✎

VAT	ID
WASP	DOA
REM	BMW
UB40	Fiat

ID is hard to categorize – it is clearly not one of the standard types of abbreviation. It's a form of IDENTITY created by apocope of the written form, and the reduced form is spelt out in letter-names, using capitals.

Discussion

VAT is variable; some people pronounce it as a single syllable (therefore it's an acronym in the narrow sense) and for some it's an initialism.

It is not always possible to categorize reduced forms firmly, as different degrees of reduction between apocope and initialism may occur. For instance, an intermediate type of reduction is found where one reduced element is represented by more than the first letter. This may well happen when the element in question is transliterated, e.g. the *Ph* in *PhD* ('doctor of philosophy') is for the Latin word *philosophiae* ('of philosophy'), with *ph* considered as representing the single Greek letter phi (φ) found in the Greek source-word.

Some words appear to be reduced forms, and historically are, but cannot be analysed as the reduced form of anything in the current state of the language. An example is MRS. (/misiz/). For many people, some of the above list will fall into the same category.

8.8 Which sorts of reduction are involved in the following expressions?

HRT	IRA	pro-am (tournament)
nimby	BSc	docudrama
camcorder	acupressure	AC/DC
ME	TLC	ROM
parascending	EFTPOS	

Discussion

As an example of how complex some of this abbreviatory activity can get, consider THE FOOTSIE. The source is the initialism FTSE ('Financial Times Stock Exchange') Index, given a pronunciation as if it were a natural word of English – in fact a play on a real one; that makes it an acronym. The acronym is then re-spelt as if it were the word on which it is a play.

ENGLISH PET-NAME FORMATION

The traditional method of forming pet-names in English was to take the base of the given-name, and to add -Y or -IE to it or to an abbreviated form of it (minor changes in spelling should be ignored here). Examples are: *John/Johnny* and *Ann/Annie*.

EXERCISES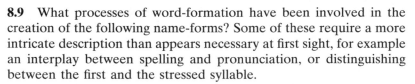

8.9 What processes of word-formation have been involved in the creation of the following name-forms? Some of these require a more intricate description than appears necessary at first sight, for example an interplay between spelling and pronunciation, or distinguishing between the first and the stressed syllable.

Stanley	Stan	Mary	Mally (but usually spelt Molly)
Peter	Pete	Virginia	Ginny
Terence	Terry, Tel	Catherine	Katie
Charles	Chas	Margaret	Maggie, Meg
Derek	Del	Frances(ca)	Frankie
Darren	Daz	Abigail	Gail
Gary	Gaz		
Anthony	Tony		
Michael	Mick, Mike		
Sylvester	Sly		

8.10 Can you think of any other examples of each of the processes you have identified?

Here is a list of words formed by abbreviation in Russian:

kolxoz	*kollektivnoe xozjajstvo*	'collective farm'
gosizdat	*gosudarstvennoe izdatel'stvo*	'state publishing-house'
politbjuro	*politicheskij bjuro*	'political office'
zapchast'	*zapasnaja chast'*	'spare part'
fizkul'tura	*fizicheskaja kul'tura*	'physical education'
vetfel'dsher	*veterinarnyj fel'dsher*	'veterinary assistant'
oblsud	*oblastnoj sud*	'district court'
profsojuz	*professional'nyj sojuz*	'trades union'

8.11 (a) What sort of expression is being reduced? (b) How many types of reduction did you identify?

Specialists in Slavic languages call these mechanisms STUB-COMPOUNDING, because, systematically, the first element is reduced to a stub of one or two syllables irrespective of the internal structure of that element.

8.12 Which English examples that you looked at above might be called stub-compounds?

8.13 What categories of abbreviations introduced earlier does stub-compounding correspond to?

- identification and naming of relations between forms with the same meaning as each other

CLIPPING (PROCOPE, APOCOPE); BLENDING; TELESCOPING; ACRONYMY; INITIALISM; STUB-COMPOUNDING

- Abbreviation is a live set of processes in everyday usage.
- Abbreviated forms may become the true or only term for a concept.

9

ALLOMORPHY: BOOKS WITH MORE THAN ONE COVER

> The fact that in most languages many morphemes appear in more than one shape.
> All the examples in this Unit and the next are from English.

In writing the previous Units of this book, I've made myself take very great care to select examples avoiding one major complication. Almost every example given so far is capable of neat analysis into separate morphemes with fixed shapes and clear boundaries (but note Exercise 7.12). However, it very common in most languages for morphemes to turn up in different shapes. Consider this example of a morpheme being pronounced in more than one way. The English verb LOVE has a derived noun-form LOVER. This has the suffix -ER which is found in very many other such derivatives: WASHER, BUILDER, HOUSE-HUNTER, and so on. But when the -ER is added, what happens to the base? It loses its final -e, leaving just *lov-*. This fact, the appearance of a morpheme in more than one shape, is called ALLOMORPHY. (We can analyse this term: ALLO- is a bound root morpheme meaning 'variant', MORPH is a morpheme meaning 'form', as we know well by now, and -Y is a noun-forming suffix meaning something like 'state, condition', as in ORTHO-DOXY; so allomorphy is 'the state of having variants in form'.) Each variant is called an ALLOMORPH. In this Unit we'll start by looking at allomorphy with regard to spelling, then go on to allomorphy with regard to pronunciation.

Allomorphy

Allomorph

    Divide the following words up into their constituent morphemes. You need to do that before you can work out which ones come in different forms.

comedy	keep	sweet	sieved
shepherd	long	conic	pigsty

drive	sweet	division	length
sieve	shop	drift	deception
cone	signed	signature	comic
pig	piggy	pork	kept
divide	deceive	divine	sheep
sign	drivel	driven	

9.1 Now pick out the pairs of words in the list containing a morpheme whose forms are related by allomorphy. Remember that the two (or more) allomorphs that you identify should be plausibly related in meaning. And affixes as well as stems and bases can show allomorphy.

EXERCISES ✎

The letters which actually distinguish the pairs of allomorphs are said to ALTERNATE with each other. You probably picked out *sheep* and *shepherd*. In this pair, *-ee-* and *-e-* alternate. *-ee-/-e-* is an ALTERNATION, and *sheep/shep-* are allomorphs. (You might prefer to respect the pattern that you can detect here and call them ALTERNANTS.)

Discussion
Alternate
Alternation

Alternants

9.2 List all the alternations that you have discovered in the word-list above.

COMEDY and COMIC are not related by allomorphy. Why not? Neither are PIG and PIGSTY. Why not? But PIG and PIGGY are. Why? DIVIDE and DIVISION are, and so are LONG and LENGTH. Why?

COMEDY and COMIC each contain a base of the same shape, with the lexical morphemes -EDY (as in TRAG-EDY) and -IC (as in TRAG-IC). PIGSTY is simply a compound, where PIG is dependent on the head STY – no variation in form can be seen. On the other hand, PIGGY contains a widespread lexical suffix -Y, which means that its base is *pigg-*; this alternates with *pig*. DIVISION is a derived form of DIVIDE; -ION is the lexical suffix, and *divide* and *divis-* alternate. Similarly, *long* alternates with *leng-*; -TH is a lexical suffix first seen in **Unit 1**.

Discussion

9.3 How many of the alternations that you have picked out can be found in other sets of words? For instance, if you had picked out a pair GYRATE and GYRATION, in the belief that the latter is GYRAT-ION, then every other pair of words whose bases end in *-ate* (verb) and *-at-* (when *-ion* is added to the base to make a noun) would be parallels.

In GYRATE/-ATION, you would have found a pattern of great generality and significance within English: DECORATE/-ATION,

Discussion

CREATE/-ATION, ELEVATE/-ATION, PREVARICATE/
-ATION, and so on. The same is true to some degree for the written
forms CONE/CON-IC: compare BASE/BAS-IC, STATE/STAT-IC,
ATHLETE/ATHLET-IC, MISANTHROPE/MISANTHROPIC
and MORPHEME/MORPHEM-IC. DIVIDE/DIVIS-ION is paral-
leled by DECIDE/DECIS-ION, DERIDE/DERIS-ION, EVADE/
EVAS-ION, ERODE/EROS-ION and quite a significant number of
others. Any other alternations you have found are likely to be
relatively restricted. The one in DECEIVE/DECEPT-ION is paral-
leled by a class of words originally sharing a root (RECEIVE,
CONCEIVE, PERCEIVE).

The most significant alternations are those where you can say that
one of the alternants appears under certain definite conditions, and
the other(s) under others. The forms with -AT- precede lexical
suffixes beginning with a vowel letter, otherwise -ATE appears: cf.
CREAT-OR, CREAT-IVE, STATE-MENT.

9.4 Below is a list of English suffixed nouns. Segment the words
into their constituent morphemes, as usual. Having taken off the
affixes, you'll notice that the base-forms are not spelt in the same
way as each other – they show allomorphy. Say exactly under what
conditions each of the two base-forms appears.

Reminder: allomorphs are variants of the same morpheme. Be careful
to distinguish allomorphy from cases where one morpheme is simply
accompanied by another. CLASS and CLASSY are not related
by allomorphy. CLASSY simply has an extra morpheme -Y, and
CLASS(-) is the same in each word. You can't look for allomorphs
until you've done your segmentation.

agile	agility	obscene	obscenity
virile	virility	grave	gravity
sublime	sublimity	sane	sanity
divine	divinity	inane	inanity
bovine	bovinity	urbane	urbanity
alkaline	alkalinity	profane	profanity
asinine	asininity	chaste	chastity
serene	serenity	deprave(d)	depravity
severe	severity		

9.5 Below is some data about the regular English plural suffix for
nouns, usually spelt -*s* or -*es*. Separate the occurrences of the -*s*
spelling from those of the -*es* spelling. Make sure you decide whether
the -*e*- in a particular instance is part of the stem or part of the suffix.
(*Hint*: how is the relevant word spelt in its singular form, i.e. without
the suffix?)

Where does the *-s* occur, and where does the *-es* occur? How regular is what you have discovered? Use other English words not in the list to test your solution.

atoms	flicks
catches	clogs
gashes	sledges
trains	turnips
fads	slabs
ghosts	dominoes
lips	bells
bullets	fellows
swings	sailors
vases	bronzes
colleges	kisses
camouflages	splints
brows	days
eyes	years
slaves	gallons
referees	streams
kangaroos	ranges
toys	flukes
potatoes	bananas
ploughs	baths

Some of our most traditional spelling rules have to do with allomorphy.

9.6 Divide up the words in the following list into their constituent morphemes, and then note those morphemes which show allomorphy. Can you make a statement which relates the different forms to each other?

scruffy	scruffily
airy	airily
portly	portlier
grumpy	grumpiest
carry	carrier
amplify	amplifier
gratify	gratification
civility	civilities

This is a point at which we can note that there are two traditions among linguists about how to describe allomorphy. The one offered in the model answer is a DISTRIBUTIONAL one: it says that one allomorph occurs under such-and-such conditions, and a different allomorph occurs under different conditions; the two allomorphs have different DISTRIBUTIONS. The other sort of answer is a PROCESSUAL

Discussion

Distributional

Distributions
Processual

Process

one. With this kind of approach, you take one of the allomorphs as basic and say it is affected by a rule or PROCESS which makes it into something else. So the processual approach would allow you to say that when a further suffix is added to a base or stem ending in -*y*, that -*y* is changed to -*i*-. (This recalls what was said in the discussion after Exercise 6.3.)

9.7   For students who have done some phonetics: why do some of the following words have a single consonant-letter in the spelling, and others a double one? (This may be hard unless you have studied phonetics, because the underlying reason for the difference in the forms used has to do with the way the words are pronounced, and is not just an effect produced within a string of letters like that in Exercise 9.5.)

When you do your initial segmentation, consider very carefully where to put the BOUNDARY.

stop	stopping	slim	slimming
tip	tipping	ram	ramming
stoop	stooping	loom	looming
sleep	sleeping	foam	foaming
gripe	griping	mime	miming
slope	sloping	assume	assuming
rob	robbing	flit	flitting
jab	jabbing	bet	betting
boob	boobing	meet	meeting
imbibe	imbibing	hoot	hooting
tube	tubing	bite	biting
rev	revving	mate	mating
drive	driving		
leave	leaving		

Discussion

The distributional way of expressing your answers would be to say that, for instance, double consonants occur under certain conditions, single ones under others, and so on. The traditional alternative way of putting it is to express it as a process: for instance, that single consonants are basic and get doubled under certain conditions.

The simplest solution to this exercise is that the double consonant-letter appears at the boundary between two morphemes where the vowel-sound in the spoken form of the first one is short; you get the single letter where the preceding vowel-sound is long. In fact, the double consonant-letter is one of the standard ways in English spelling of marking the fact that the pronunciation of the preceding vowel is short. This operates in addition to the rule that we noted in Exercise 9.4 about the presence or absence of -*e* at the end of the stem.

9.8   When we segment the words, why would it be better to draw the boundary after the pair of double letters, instead of between them?

If we do it after the pair, we are committed to the belief that there is allomorphy of the stem, i.e. that the stem appears in more than one form (e.g. *stop* and *stopp-*).

    If we do it between them, that makes the second instance a part of the suffix. In this second instance, we are committed to saying that the *-ing* suffix can come in all sorts of shapes, such as *-ping*, *-bing*, *-ving* and so on, and that the choice of which to use depends on what the final consonant of the stem was. So we might just as well attach the second consonant to the stem anyway, and have a universal suffix *-ing* which does not itself show allomorphy even if it causes allomorphy of the stem to which it gets attached.

    This solution shows again the importance to linguists of making statements in their analyses which have the greatest possible degree of generality, and the fewest exceptions, oddities and special cases.

Discussion

Sometimes we find that allomorphy is related to principles of the structure of the language we're investigating. In the data we looked at in Exercise 9.4, for example, there were lots of words ending with the noun-forming morpheme -ITY. Now it's a general fact about English spelling that -ITY can't be added to a base ending in *-e* without an effect on that base, and it's a general fact about English pronunciation that certain long vowels are forbidden in the last syllable of a stem when followed by -ITY. (OBESITY may represent an exception for some speakers, and it is a troubling one. Other exceptions are indicated by spelling devices: note NICETY and VARIETY where the suffix is spelt *-ety*.)

    Some spelling-allomorphy is completely general. There are no exceptions to the rule that says that stems must not end in a consonant-letter plus *-e* when the suffix *-ing* is added (thus *date/dating*, and so on). This can be generalized. A final *-e* after a consonant-letter never survives when an affix beginning with an *i* or *e* is added. The apparent exception, SWINGEING, is arguably not complex at all, as SWINGE doesn't exist as a verb in Present Day English.

PRINCIPLED ALLOMORPHY

Sometimes we find allomorphy that cannot be explained as being due to the structure of the language being investigated. In general, this happens when there used to be a pronunciation-based reason for the differences in form, but that reason has disappeared. Consider the following nouns – divide them up into morphemes, as usual.

CASUAL ALLOMORPHY

EXERCISES ✎   **9.9** Make a statement about the allomorphy of the stems of the words below.

oaf	oaves	leaf	leaves
loaf	loaves	sheaf	sheaves
roof	rooves	thief	thieves
hoof	hooves	wharf	wharves
wife	wives	dwarf	dwarves
knife	knives	calf	calves
life	lives	half	halves
beef	beeves	wolf	wolves

Discussion   If you are a very conservative English-speaker – and you almost certainly aren't – you will spell the words in the right-hand columns with -*ve* (and pronounce them with a /v/ sound). If not, you will use an -*f*. Note especially, for instance, whether you say *roofs* not *rooves*.

You've probably finished up with a list which is by no means as regular as the situation I originally presented. You may, for instance, say *loaves* and *leaves*, but *roofs*. That is, some of your stems finish with the traditional -*ve*, and others with the same -*f* or -*fe* that you find in the singular. All those words which are in your -*f* list have lost allomorphy – there is no difference between the form of the stem of the singular and that of the plural. That's because there is in English no structural pressure for them to vary; there are other similar nouns which have never had such allomorphy of the stem, such as *fife* and *safe* (i.e. 'strongbox'), or lost it so long ago that there is no impact on Modern English, like *cliff*. There are also plenty of words with -*ve* in both the singular and the plural, like *sleeve* and *wave*. So English clearly had no overriding principle demanding that singular nouns had -*f(e)* and plural nouns -*ve*. Accordingly, its writers have been busy getting rid of the allomorphy in these words, with only the more frequently-used ones still following the older pattern for most people. The smaller your number of words in the -*ve* category, the more progressive you are as a speaker of English. That doesn't mean that what you do is either good or bad – it's just an indication of the direction of an ongoing change in English.

Where there is allomorphy for no structural reason, then, change in the language tends to remove it.

9.10 Below is a list of some intimately-related pairs of words. Segment each multi-morpheme word in the right-hand column of each pair first; one of its morphemes is frequently seen or heard (i.e. in speech and/or writing), in the word concerned, in a different form from the one stated.

What in each instance is the different form? And can you explain what is going on? What is related to what by allomorphy, in each instance?

dream	dreamt	wreak	wrought (as in wreak havoc)
burn	burnt	beseech	besought
learn	learnt	bereave	bereft
spell	spelt	formula	formulae
spoil	spoilt	index	indices
kneel	knelt	brother	brethren
leap	leapt	pronounce	pronunciation

Discussion

If I'm right about what's happening in your English, any 'different' form is gradually replacing the one listed in the exercise. It will also be more regular than the one in the data-set, in that it will not show the allomorphy which is visible or audible in that one. You may not be consistent about whether you use a form from the data-set or an alternative to it. You may use your two alternatives, such as *dreamt* and *dreamed*, in different styles: *dreamed* may seem less literary and more spontaneous than *dreamt*, and *indices* may seem more appropriate in technical writing whilst *indexes* seems better in speech.

9.11   A recap – a deceptively simple-looking problem: the indefinite article in English comes in two allomorphs, *a* and *an*, as in *a row* as opposed to *an argument*. When is which one used?

VARIATION IN THE SPOKEN FORM OF MORPHEMES

Written allomorphy
Spoken allomorphy

So far we've concentrated on WRITTEN ALLOMORPHY. But SPOKEN ALLOMORPHY is also possible. You'll have an advantage in this part of the Unit if you've done some phonetics and phonology, but I'll keep technicality to a minimum and explain anything crucial to understanding the data I present. You will need to take care to notice that there is not necessarily a one-to-one relation between the facts of pronunciation and the facts of writing, because the spelling-system of English is not designed simply to represent significant pronunciation differences.

Consider the noun HOUSE in its plural form *houses*. The written form is analysable with ease: we have a one-morpheme stem *house*, and a plural suffix *-s*. However, this disguises a difference in pronunciation in the stem itself. The singular form is pronounced with an /s/ sound at the end; the stem of the plural form is pronounced with a /z/ sound before the suffix: *hou*/s/*e* and *hou*/z/*e-s*.

Some of the words in the data-set of Exercise 9.1 are found to be related by allomorphy when you consider their pronunciation, as opposed to their spelling. A good instance is SIGN and SIGNATURE. The root is spelt the same in both words; but it isn't pronounced the same. There is spoken allomorphy but not written allomorphy.

In the case of -ATE and -ATION, note also the change in pronunciation in the verb stem that is a consequence of adding the noun-marker -ION. The /t/ alternates with /ʃ/, the initial sound in *ship*. Notice again that one allomorph appears under one set of conditions (i.e. before the suffix), and the other under different ones (i.e. not before the suffix).

EXERCISE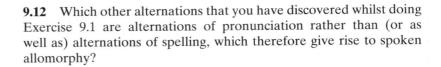

9.12 Which other alternations that you have discovered whilst doing Exercise 9.1 are alternations of pronunciation rather than (or as well as) alternations of spelling, which therefore give rise to spoken allomorphy?

Some allomorphy is clearly principled, that is, explainable, as we saw above, whilst some is not. There is no simple explanation for the facts about HOUSE that I discussed above without embarking on the story of the way English pronunciation has changed over the last 1000 years or so. Let's start with something easier to grasp.

One English lexical negative prefix is usually spelt *in-*, as in:

inactive   interminable   inopportune   indecisive

This is an accurate reflection of its pronunciation. However, the same negative prefix is pronounced /im-/, and spelt accordingly, in some words, for instance: *immobile, improbable, impotent, imbalance*.

The prefix therefore shows allomorphy: it has two forms. There is a clear reason for this, though. The form *im-* only occurs where the following root begins with a consonant articulated with the closure of both lips: /m/, /p/, /b/, and it occurs there on every possible occasion. The reason for the variation is easy to state, and it has an explanation in pronunciation: /im-/, ending in a consonant produced with lip-closure, before another consonant produced with lip-closure; /in-/ everywhere else. Actually, the situation is a little more complex in speech than in writing, because in addition *in-* is pronounced with an /ŋ/ sound (as at the end of *thing*), where the base begins with a /k/ or /g/ sound: *inclement, ingratitude*. The /ŋ/ sound, the /k/ and the /g/ are all produced with the same kind of closure, one involving the back of the tongue and the soft palate at the back of the roof of the mouth. The explanation for this third different pronunciation of *in-* is therefore just like that for *im-*: it depends on the pronunciation of the consonant at the beginning of the base.

ENGLISH NOUN PLURALS: ALLOMORPHY OF SPOKEN FORMS

Go back to the data-set of Exercise 9.5. Consider carefully how the suffix is pronounced in each word. It may be pronounced /z/, /s/ or /iz/, as in *bags*, *backs* and *badges* respectively. Make a list of the sounds which occur at the end of the stem, immediately before the suffix. Remember that sounds and letters aren't the same thing

– there isn't always a clear relation between the two in English spelling. For example, *maze* and *vase* end in the same sound, /z/; *yes* and *as* don't. Concentrate on the pronunciation.

9.13 Can you discover what leads it to show this allomorphy? Is the solution tidier or less tidy than the one you achieved when you were looking at the spelling-allomorphy?

EXERCISES ✎

If you have no knowledge of phonetics, simply listing the sounds occurring before each different form of the suffix will lead to an answer which is an adequate description of the facts of English. From a knowledge of phonetics, you may be able to give a more sophisticated explanation of what determines which pronunciation is used by considering the notions of sibilance and assimilation. The form of the suffix is determined as follows: a vowel /i/ or /ə/ (it depends on the speaker's accent which of these is chosen) is inserted after the stem if it ends in a sibilant; the fricative consonant forming the suffix is then either voiced or voiceless depending on whether what immediately precedes it is voiced or voiceless (i.e. it assimilates in voicing to its preceding segment).

Discussion

Some conservative speakers of English show an alternation which can best be approached through the spelling of the relevant words. These speakers pronounce /h/ in the words beginning with *h*- in the contexts in the left-hand column below, but don't do so in the corresponding positions in the right-hand column.

9.14 Account for the use and non-use of /h/ by these speakers.

a history	an historic event
a house	an hotel
a heron	an hereditary peer
a hero	an heroic effort
a habit	an habitual drunkard
horizontal	horizon
heretic	heretical
Helen	St Helena (the island in the Atlantic)

9.15 What completely general principle is illustrated by the following data? Say the words aloud if you are unsure – this is a question of pronunciation only. (Ignore the small complications created by the letters in brackets.)

mason	masonic	German	Germanic
poet	poetic	diplomat	diplomatic
sulphur	sulphuric	telephon(e)	telephonic
econom(y)	economic	alcohol	alcoholic

histor(y)	historic	photograph	photographic
metal	metal(l)ic	robot	robotic
iron(y)	ironic	atmospher(e)	atmospheric
anarch(y)	anarchic	thermostat	thermostatic
despot	despotic	melod(y)	melodic
astronom(y)	astronomic	colon	colonic
atom	atomic	athlet(e)	athletic

(*Hint*: there is actually one inexplicable exception – *Arab/Arabic*.)

9.16   What does the general rule predict for the pronunciation of *Arabic*?

Discussion

If you have an acute ear, you will have noticed that this affects the pronunciation of the vowels also. It creates alternations, in many instances, between a full vowel and a reduced or neutral vowel /ə/, pronounced like the *-a* in *Emma*. The full vowel occurs when stressed, and the /ə/ when not stressed. Try this out in *atom/atomic*.

9.17   Why do the following words appear not to follow the pattern we've identified?

turmeric	heretic
bishopric	catholic
biopic	lunatic

OUTCOMES OF UNIT 9

Skills learnt

- identification of alternants
- identification and description of patterns in English, including identifying the conditions under which particular allomorphs appear

Terms learnt

ALLOMORPHY, ALLOMORPH; ALTERNATION, ALTERNATE, ALTERNANT; DISTRIBUTION; PROCESS; PRINCIPLED and CASUAL ALLOMORPHY; WRITTEN and SPOKEN ALLOMORPHY; SIBILANCE; ASSIMILATION

Principles learnt

- Allomorphy involves variant forms of the same unit.
- Allomorphs may occur under specific conditions, such as before certain letters or before certain suffixes.
- Allomorphy affects spoken as well as written forms.
- Solutions maximizing generality and minimizing exceptionality are preferred.
- Under certain conditions, allomorphy may disappear over time in the interests of simplicity or generality.

Topics further practised

- segmentation and classification

ALLOMORPHY IN OTHER LANGUAGES

10

> In most languages many morphemes appear in more than one shape.
> All the examples are from languages other than English.

Now some examples from languages other than English. In each case, we explore the reasons for the variation in form of some morpheme. A number of the data-sets and their solutions will make greater sense if you have done courses in phonetics and phonology, but I'll try to keep technicalities to a minimum, as in **Unit 9**, and explain the phenomena before asking you to think about the data. However, forms will be given in written or transliterated form in the case of standardized written languages, not the IPA alphabet. The first two sections consist of worked examples with no questions on them.

A very frequent reason for allomorphy is that some fact about the pronunciation of adjacent elements has an impact on the shape of the element you are examining. Consider the following simple case of vowel-harmony.

PRONUNCIA-TION-BASED REASONS FOR ALLOMORPHY

Tatar is a Turkic language, controversially assigned to the Altaic family, spoken mainly in the Tatar Republic of Asiatic Russia.

Tatar

an	'mother'	*an-am*	'my mother'
qiz	'daughter'	*qiz-im*	'my daughter'
qol	'leg'	*qol-um*	'my leg'
palytor	'coat'	*palytor-um*	'my coat'
almi-lir	'apple-s'	*almi-lir-im*	'my apples'

Note the forms of the possessive suffix meaning 'my'. Which vowel appears in it is dictated by the nature of the vowel or vowels in the stem. It is an approximate copy of (on this data) the last one in the stem: /a/ and /i/ yield copies, whilst /o/ requires /u/.

Korean

Korean is a language whose family relations are uncertain, but some linguists associate it with Japanese and with the Altaic family.

Here we also find that the nature of particular sound-units has a decisive effect on the sound-structure of adjacent ones, but in a different sort of way. The suffix -to means 'also'; let's consider its effect on the root to which it is attached. (Note that ch, ch', p' and t' should each be treated as representing single units of sound.)

ap'-	'front'	ap-to		nach-	'daytime'	nat-to
kaps-	'price'	kap-to		pat'-	'garden'	pat-to
os-	'clothes'	ot-to		pakk-	'outside'	pak-to
kkoch'-	'flower'	kkot-to		talk-	'chicken'	tak-to

Any root ending in a labial consonant or consonant cluster (p', ps) is pronounced with the labial /p/; any with a dental or palatal (s, ch', ch, t') pronounced with the dental /t/; and any with a velar (kk, lk) as the velar /k/. Only /p/, /t/ and /k/ are permitted before /t/ within a morpheme, and if the root to which -to is attached ends in a different consonant, or a cluster, it is made to conform. This illustrates the impact of strings of consonants permitted inside a morpheme; where morphemes come together, their consonants are made to behave as they would within a morpheme. The result is allomorphy of the stem.

Luganda

Here is a simple problem concerning words in Luganda (a Bantu language of the Niger-Congo family, spoken in East Africa), all except the first two borrowed from other languages. They all contain the noun-class prefix en- seen in enjovu 'elephant'.

EXERCISE ✎

10.1 Describe the formation of these word-forms below. Why is this question in a Unit about allomorphy?

empiso	'needle'	eŋŋoma	'drum'
ekkooti	'coat'	emmotoka	'car'
essowaani	'plate'	essanduuko	'box'
edduuka	'shop'	ebbakuli	'bowl'
eggaali	'bike'	ettawaaza	'hurricane lamp'

Classical Nahuatl

Classical Nahuatl was the official language of the former Aztec empire in Mexico (Uto-Aztecan family).

There is a special grammatical category in Nahuatl which is expressed as a suffix on noun stems to make them fully usable sentences: it means roughly 'it is'. For instance, the root morpheme meaning 'tomato' in Nahuatl is TOMA- (literally meaning 'fat thing'). Like all other similar ones, it is bound; it cannot be said alone, but only in contexts translatable into English as complete sentences. Most obviously we find things like *nimitztomamacaz*, i.e. *ni-mitz-toma-maca-z*, literally 'I-to you-tomato-give-future', i.e. 'I'll give you a tomato'. If you want to say 'tomato' in isolation, you have to equip the stem with the suffix mentioned, thus *toma-tl*, literally translatable by an English sentence, not a word: 'It's a tomato' (This is the form which gives us, via Spanish, our word *tomato*.)

The singular version of this suffix comes in different shapes, /-tl/, /-tli/, /-li/ (cf. Exercise 7.10).

EXERCISE ✎

10.2 What do you consider to be the factor(s) causing the alternation? (Note that the colon (:) is a sign of a long preceding vowel.)

mi:-tl	'arrow'	*mix-tli*	'puma'
iye-tl	'tobacco'	*wi:lo:-tl*	'dove'
peyo-tl	'type of cactus'	*tepe:-tl*	'mountain'
cih-tli	'hare'	*nopal-li*	'type of cactus'
mix-tli	'cloud'	*te:uc-tli*	'lord'
coyo:-tl	'wolf'	*cuauh-tli*	'eagle'
pil-li	'nobleman, child'	*petz-tli*	'fool's gold'
toma-tl	'tomato'	*xi:hui-tl*	'comet'
tecpin-tli	'flea'	*xochi-tl*	'flower'
papah-tli	'tousled long hair'	*cihua:-tl*	'woman'
oquich-tli	'man'	*xa:l-li*	'sand'
na:wa-tl	'person speaker of Nahuatl'	*tzapo-tl*	'sapote tree'
to:p-tli	'idol'	*co:a:-tl*	'snake'
po:c-tli	'smoke'		

Discussion

Obviously the choice of a form in /l/ next to a form in /l/ is not an accident; in such instances the suffixal /-tl/ is said to ASSIMILATE to the /l/ terminating the stem, i.e. to appear in a form more like it than that which appears elsewhere (cf. the solution to Exercise 9.15).

St Lucia French Creole

This creole language is spoken on the formerly British West Indian island of St Lucia.

EXERCISES ✎

10.3 Explain the alternating forms of the definiteness marker below (the last morpheme in each expression). The data is slightly simplified.

volɛ ja	'the thief'	*bagaj la*	'the thing'
bug la	'the bloke'	*ʃimẽ jã*	'the way'

lekɔl la	'the school'	*ku a*	'the blow'
lapas la	'the market'	*ʃipi ja*	'the doorstep'
bɛf la	'the cow'	*tɛt la*	'the head'
maʃin na	'the machine'	*fi ja*	'the daughter'
mun na	'the person'	*misie ja*	'the gentleman'
kɔn na	'the horn'	*fɛj la*	'the leaf'
mãsõʒ na	'the lie'	*maʒɛstra a*	'the magistrate'
madam na	'the lady'	*prɛt la*	'the priest'
ʃam na	'the room'	*mamaj la*	'the child'
lãŋ na	'the tongue'	*rimɛd la*	'the medicine'
ʃapo a	'the hat'	*betʃe ja*	'the white man'
kaj la	'the house'	*vã ã*	'the wind'
tʃyizin na	'the kitchen'	*mɔn na*	'the hill'

10.4   What form of the definiteness marker would you predict to occur after the following nouns:

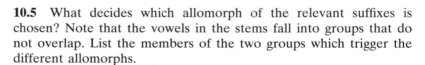

dʒab	devil	*hɔ̃t*	shame
jam	yam	*lamɔ*	death
kɔminiõ	communion	*plãtɛ*	planter

Hungarian

Hungarian is one of the two main European languages of the Finno-Ugric family, the other being Finnish.

In Hungarian, nouns have a range of suffixes for case and number whose form varies according to which vowel or vowels appear in the stem.

EXERCISES

10.5   What decides which allomorph of the relevant suffixes is chosen? Note that the vowels in the stems fall into groups that do not overlap. List the members of the two groups which trigger the different allomorphs.

stem	dative singular ('to')	ablative singular ('from')
ház 'house'	*háznak*	*háztól*
város 'town'	*városnak*	*várostól*
kutya 'dog'	*kutyanak*	*kutyatól*
szoba 'room'	*szobanak*	*szobatól*
mérnök 'engineer'	*mérnöknek*	*mérnöktől*
tömeg 'crowd'	*tömegnek*	*tömegtől*
könyv 'book'	*könyvnek*	*könyvtől*
fö 'head'	*fönek*	*fötől*

If you have taken a course in phonetics and phonology, you will be able to answer this question in a fuller and more explanatory way; cf. the exposition above of the Tatar data (page 73).

The following forms appear to present a problem, but it can be cleared up by adopting one extra principle.

10.6   What extra principle is needed to account for them? (A minor complication has been removed from some of them.)

béka 'frog'	*békanak*	*békától*
tányér 'plate'	*tányérnak*	*tányértól*
csillag 'star'	*csillagnak*	*csillagtól*

Stems with back (Group 1) vowels (which include /a/ in Hungarian) take back-vowelled allomorphs of the suffixes, and stems with front (Group 2) take front-vowelled allomorphs. Where the principles conflict, as in the extra three words, back-vowelled forms win out and trigger back-vowelled allomorphs. (That's the extra principle: back vowels win.)   **Discussion**

10.7   Why is the following data problematic?

cél 'aim'	*célnak*	*céltól*
kép 'picture'	*képnek*	*képtől*
kert 'garden'	*kertnek*	*kerttől*
híd 'bridge'	*hídnak*	*hídtól*
szín 'colour'	*színnek*	*színtől*

The obvious way of doing this is simply to say they are marked in the lexicon (and in real-world dictionaries of Hungarian) as selecting back-vowelled (Group 1) allomorphs even though the stems have front (Group 2) vowels.   **Discussion**

Some linguists prefer a different, more abstract, style of analysis (see the discussion after Exercise 6.3), by which they treat the exceptional words as having back (Group 1) vowels at some deep level of analysis, and convert these distinct back vowels into front (Group 2) vowels after the selection of the relevant allomorphs. Both styles of analysis have their adherents.

10.8   In the longer term, remembering the English data-set of Exercise 9.12, what do you think might happen to such exceptions such as 'aim' and 'bridge'?

There is evidence that exceptions have become regular. For example, SZIRT ('cliff') used to take unexpected back-vowelled suffixes and now takes the expected front-vowelled ones. This might come to affect the exceptional instances here also.   **Discussion**

10.9 Work out the Hungarian for 'to friends' and 'from a wife', given *barát-ok* ('friend-s') and *feleség* ('wife') and assuming they are not exceptional.

10.10 The delative case (meaning 'from the top of') is represented by a suffix with the two allomorphs *-ról* and *-ről*. What would you expect the Hungarian to be for 'from the top of a house', 'garden', and 'bridge'?

Often the reasons for allomorphy are only partly to do with pronunciation, as we shall see in some data-sets below. The Hungarian data suggests that simple exceptionality has to be reckoned with, and there are other reasons too.

German

One of the the abstract-noun-forming suffixes of German alternates in shape between *-heit* and *-keit*.

schlaff	'slack'	*Schlaffheit* 'slackness' (and so on)
ge-sell-ig	'sociable'	*Geselligkeit*
ge-müt-lich	'matey'	*Gemütlichkeit*
lang-sam	'slow'	*Langsamkeit*
faul	'lazy'	*Faulheit*
träg(e)	'idle'	*Trägheit* 'inertia'
zahm	'tame'	*Zahmheit*
gerad(e)	'straight'	*Geradheit*
weich	'soft, tender'	*Weichheit*
weich-lich	'tender'	*Weichlichkeit*
schlau	'sly'	*Schlauheit*
flach	'flat'	*Flachheit*
tapfer	'brave'	*Tapferkeit*
brauch-bar	'useful'	*Brauchbarkeit*
dunkel	'dark'	*Dunkelheit*
sicher	'secure'	*Sicherheit*
be-währ-t	'tried and trusted'	*Bewährtheit*
eitel	'vain'	*Eitelkeit*

Where the base adjective has structure of its own, I have marked it by hyphenation.

EXERCISE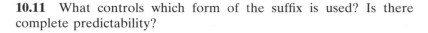

10.11 What controls which form of the suffix is used? Is there complete predictability?

Discussion

The main body of the solution has to do with the shape, including the pronunciation or spelling, of the base adjective. Does your solution come out exceptionless? If not, where does any difficulty lie? Are the reasons for the allomorphy completely to do with the pronunciation of the bases?

There are some principles involved. Only *-keit* appears after a suffix, which is not a matter of pronunciation at all, but of word-structure; *-heit* seems to be preferred in most other cases – in fact in all instances where the base adjective has only one syllable, which is a question of pronunciation. Two-syllable bases that are not morphologically complex are a problem – we find *Dunkelheit* and *Eitelkeit*, and no principle will explain why a particular allomorph of our suffix is chosen. Clearly it is not just about how the base is pronounced.

French

Some of the data-sets you have worked through so far show abundant evidence that the shape of elements may vary depending on the other elements or words that accompany them. The reasons for such variation may include the pronunciation of key adjacent elements; or simply which words are involved, irrespective of their pronunciation. Consider the singular definite articles in French, *le* and *la* (masculine and feminine respectively); both have an alternative form *l'*.

le stylo	'the pen'
le train	'the train'
le visage	'the face'
la croix	'the cross'
la nuit	'the night
la lutte	'the struggle'
le avare → l'avare	'the miser'
le ivrogne → l'ivrogne	'the drunkard'
le outil → l'outil	'the tool'
la expression → l'expression	'the expression'
la onde → l'onde	'the wave'
la université → l'université	'the university'

EXERCISE

10.12   What is the reason for this, to judge by this data?

Discussion

That it's to do with pronunciation appears to be shown by the behaviour of *le* and *la* with words beginning with *h*, which is silent in French:

le habit → l'habit	'the costume'
le horizon → l'horizon	'the horizon'
la habitude → l'habitude	'the custom'
la heure → l'heure	'the hour'

This results in the cancellation of the visible and audible distinction between feminine and masculine in one group of words.

There are significant exceptions to this behaviour with silent *h*, though. We find:

le heurt	'the bump, knock'
le houx	'the holly'
le hasard	'chance'
la hernie	'the rupture'
la houppe	'the tuft'
la hache	'the axe'

There is no way of distinguishing the words in this data-set from *habit* and *heure*; they both begin with vowel sounds. So we must conclude that they fail to demand the form *l'* of the definite article for no other reason than because they are the words they are. We find *le heurt* and not **l'heurt* simply because we are dealing with the word *heurt*. In other words, the choice of *l'* is not simply due to whether a vowel-sound follows it – the actual word that follows is a significant factor.

Welsh

In this data from Welsh, we see alternation in the initial consonant of some nouns.

cefn	'back'	*ei gefn e*	'his back'	*ei chefn hi*	'her back'
tafod	'tongue'	*ei dafod e*	'his tongue'	*ei thafod hi*	'her tongue'
pen	'head'	*ei ben e*	'his head'	*ei phen hi*	'her head'
gwallt	'hair'	*ei wallt e*	'his hair'	*ei gwallt hi*	'her hair'
drws	'door'	*ei ddrws e*	'his door'	*ei drws hi*	'her door'
bys	'finger'	*ei fys e*	'his finger'	*ei bys hi*	'her finger'
nerf	'nerve'	*ei nerf e*	'his nerve'	*ei nerf hi*	'her nerve'

y cefn	'the back'	*clust*	'ear'	*y glust*	'the ear'
y tafod	'the tongue'	*troed*	'foot'	*y droed*	'the foot'
y pen	'the head'	*potel*	'bottle'	*y botel*	'the bottle'
y gwallt	'the hair'	*gwefus*	'lip'	*y wefus*	'the lip'
y drws	'the door'	*dinas*	'town'	*y ddinas*	'the town'
y bys	'the finger'	*barn*	'opinion'	*y farn*	'the opinion'
y nerf	'the nerve'	*neges*	'errand'	*y neges*	'the errand

EXERCISE

10.13 Is the alternation due to the meaning of the preceding word, or to the way that word is pronounced?

Discussion

Since the shape of the words for 'his' and 'her' – or at least those parts of them that go before the noun – is identical, the effect on the initial consonant must be due to whether it's the 'his'-word or the 'her'-word. That is, the effect comes from the word chosen, not from its pronunciation.

Similarly, 'the' is rendered consistently in this data as *y*. Some of these *y* appear to have no effect on the following word (*y cefn*) whilst others do (*y glust*). This is a slightly more tortuous example of the responsibility of arbitrary sets of words for the creation of allomorphy (CASUAL ALLOMORPHY; see **Unit 9**). Welsh nouns alternate after the article in the way illustrated by the second data-set if they are grammatically feminine (CLUST*)*; they remain in the basic shape if they are masculine (CEFN). This time, the seeds of alternation are within the noun itself. The article provides the potential for the alternation to take place, but the potential can only be activated if the noun has feminine gender. In any case, the alternation has clearly got nothing to do with the pronunciation of *y*, which is the same with all nouns.

Sometimes we find aspects of word structure that appear to be entirely random and we can't explain them, except through delving into historical knowledge that isn't available to native speakers of any language without academic training in the subject. Within a lexical category, there may be several different patterns of word-structure. In Chichewa, we find a relationship between two forms of the verb called the active infinitive and the causative infinitive. The latter, the meaning of which is illustrated in the data-set below, is formed by suffixation from the stem of the former. (The -*a* ending each word is a further suffix, so we are not looking at an instance of infixation.) But which suffix is chosen seems to be a random matter.

CHOICE OF AFFIX

10.14 Chichewa is the dominant language of Malawi, and belongs to the Bantu subfamily of the Niger-Congo family. List the allomorphs of the stem below, and the allomorphs of the causative suffix. (Note: -*a* is a further suffix.)

EXERCISES ✎

Active infinitive		Causative infinitive	
kugwáda	'to kneel'	*kugwádiça*	'to cause to kneel'
kukúmba	'to dig'	*kukúmbiça*	'to cause to dig'
kubúntha	'to become blunt'	*kubúntica*	'to blunt'
kukána	'to refuse'	*kukániza*	'to cause to refuse'
kusúngga	'to protect'	*kusúnggiza*	'to cause to protect'
kutháβa	'to run away'	*kuthávya*	'to cause to run away'
kuwɔ́pa	'to fear'	*kuwɔ́fya*	'to frighten'

Some verbs appear to require a suffix -*ic*, others a suffix -*iz*, and still others a suffix -*y* which has the further effect of modifying the consonant at the end of the stem. The conclusion from this is that lexemes in the same lexical class may belong to different sub-groups (cf. **Unit 2**); the members of each sub-group may behave in similar ways to each other, but differently from members of other sub-groups.

Discussion

10.15 Which concept that you have already met is the one describing the groups that the Chichewa verbs fall into?

German

10.16   What principle decides how a verb in the data below forms its past participle form?

infinitive form	past participle form	meaning
schlingen	*geschlungen*	'to devour'
singen	*gesungen*	'to sing'
be-dingen	*be-dingt*	'to condition'
ringen	*gerungen*	'to wrestle'
bringen	*gebracht*	'to bring'
hinken	*gehinkt*	'to limp'
sinken	*gesunken*	'to sink'
schminken	*geschminkt*	'to put makeup on'
winken	*gewinkt*	'to beckon'
stinken	*gestunken*	'to stink'

Discussion

A budding German-speaker, native or not, just has to learn which verb does what. All we can do is group the verbs into morphological classes (cf. **Unit 2**). This is a recurrent feature of morphology in very many languages.

The fact that there are patterns in a language's system that cannot be fully explained is not a source of despair. First, there are many that can be explained, like some of the pronunciation-based ones illustrated in this Unit. Second, it is part of the business of a linguist to provide accurate descriptions of languages, and that goal is not the same as explanation. Third, all patterns are in principle capable of being explained historically, i.e. it can be understood how they got into a particular state even if it is unclear how or why they maintain themselves in that state.

OUTCOMES OF UNIT 10

Skills learnt

- application of skills learnt for English to data from other languages

Terms learnt

The following PHONOLOGICAL and PHONETIC concepts are mentioned: VOWEL-HARMONY; ASSIMILATION; FRONT and BACK VOWELS

They may be checked in R.L. Trask, *A dictionary of phonetics and phonology* (Routledge, 1996).

Principles learnt

- Allomorphy can arise from the effects of sound-units adjacent to the morpheme in question.
- Some allomorphy is regular, and some is exceptional.
- Some allomorphy arises from the nature of an adjacent unit, as opposed to from its pronunciation.
- Some allomorphy cannot be fully explained; but it can be accurately described.

Topic further practised

- stating distributions of allomorphs

WHERE NEXT?

In the 'Using this book' section right at the beginning I mentioned some other books in the same series as this one which will help you to continue your interest in facts of language related to word structure and help you to get a broad introductory picture of the way languages work.

Here are some suggested readings to carry on your study of word structure using deeper and more technical literature, such as you will need to read on university-level courses.

A lot of the material in this book is English, and you can usefully pursue this in greater depth in Laurie Bauer's *English word-formation* (Cambridge University Press, 1983). Bauer has also written *Introducing linguistic morphology* (Edinburgh University Press, 1988), which will help ease you into more difficult material.

Some introductory textbooks of general linguistics contain substantial sections on morphology, such as Victoria Fromkin and Robert Rodman, *An introduction to language* (Harcourt Brace, 6th edition, 1998), Chapter 3, which is about as easy as the more simple material in the present book and contains some similar exercises.

Probably the best introductory textbook which covers roughly the same ground as my present workbook is P.H. Matthews, *Morphology* (Cambridge University Press Textbooks in Linguistics, 2nd edition, 1991). An introductory textbook which covers the material of this book and also deals with some aspects of theoretical debate in morphology is Francis Katamba, *Morphology* (Macmillan Modern Linguistics, 1993).

'Theory' in morphology has to do with such questions as the following:

- How does morphology interact with other areas of language such as syntax and phonology? For instance, to understand the structure of some particular word, do you need to have access to phonological or syntactic information about the word or its neighbours?

- Is it possible to construct a single framework within which the morphology of all the world's languages can be described? For example, are there sets of languages like the Turkish, Latin and Arabic that you saw in **Units 6** and **7** so radically different that you have to conclude that there are two or more types of language?
- If a single framework is possible, what does it look like? For instance, do the rules of word structure have to apply in a certain order or not? Are there limits to the amount of allomorphy that a paradigm can tolerate?
- Is morphology the same as syntax, i.e. is it just grammar that applies within the word? Do phrases in some language have the same overall structure as words, in any sense?
- Is the distinction between inflection and derivation really necessary, or do these two aspects of word structure boil down to the same sort of thing?
- Can different approaches, with different insights, be reconciled?

A good survey of different approaches to morphology is Andrew Carstairs-McCarthy, *Current morphology* (Routledge Linguistic Theory Guides, 1992). Andrew Spencer's *Morphological theory* (Blackwell, 1991) is a massive comprehensive survey of both general theory and different approaches. Both these last two books are difficult, and you will need to master some groundwork before using them.

David Crystal's *The Cambridge encyclopedia of language* (Cambridge University Press, 2nd edition, 1997), has a particularly useful brief section on some of the issues we haven't had space to go into here, such as the definition of grammatical categories like mood and case. An excellent technical dictionary covering morphology and related areas is also available: R.L. Trask, *A dictionary of grammatical terms in linguistics* (Routledge, 1993).

ANSWERS TO EXERCISES

Note: → means 'return to text for discussion'.

1.1 →

1.2 Bound: *-y, -ed, -(e)r, -ance, -ly, dis-, -ful, un-, -ment, -ing, -ry, -(e)n, in-, -ness, -al, -ity, -ion, -(a)n, -est, re-, -less, -'s, -age*. The rest are free.

1.3 *un-bias-ed, use-(e)r-name, mort-al-ity, hope-less-ly*

1.4 →

1.5 The words in the left column can be divided up into more than one morpheme. In some instances, you might be uncertain where in the string of letters to draw the boundary between them, but you'll be certain that there should be one, wherever it goes. The ones on the right cannot sensibly be divided up into strings of morphemes at all: they are one-morpheme words.

1.6 By a strict application of the definition of morpheme offered, they're all one-morpheme words except *warmth* (*warm* plus the morpheme *-th*, which has noun-forming as its function or 'meaning' and which RECURS in *length, depth, width*, etc.).

1.7 Maybe 'small'.

1.8 →

1.9 The morphemes are *-nohe* 'mother', *-pohe* 'father', *-ro* 'hit', *-me* ' give', *-hnon* 'head', *maah* 'house', *-nta* 'for', *ti-* 'me, my', *a-* 'you/your' or 'him/his or her'. If you're really motoring, you will have split the first two in the above list of morphemes as *-ohe* 'first ascending generation ancestor', *-n-* 'female', *-p-* 'male'.

1.10   Replace the first *o* or *e* with *i* and add *-i* in final position.

1.11   Respectively, *aglu-* 'work', *aquj-* 'walk without direction', *igliχti-* 'walk', *qilpiχ-* 'make holes in', *qava-* 'sleep', *kuːjma-* 'swim', *Liŋaχta-* 'ring'.

1.12   *-quq*

UNIT 2
WORDS AND
PARADIGMS

2.1   Four written and two spoken – but read the Discussion that follows Exercise 2.2.

2.2   Four, written and spoken – but read the Discussion that follows.

2.3   How about BE and SING respectively?

2.4   (It's not important here to get the technical terms right. Just check your observations.)

present simple	*beat*
present 3rd person singular	*beats*
infinitive/imperative	*beat*
past simple	*beat*
present participle	*beating*
past/passive participle	*beaten*

Note the differences from PLAY. No new principles or categories are needed.

2.5

present 1st person singular	*am*
present 2nd person singular	*are*
present 3rd person singular	*is*
present plural	*are*
infinitive/imperative	*be*
past simple singular (not 2nd person)	*was*
past simple plural and 2nd person singular	*were*
present participle	*being*
past/passive participle	*been*

New principles concerning person and number are needed. →

2.6   2 SG, 'tense' 1: *audis*; 1 PL, 'tense' 2: *audiverimus*; 2 PL, 'tense' 2: *audiveritis*; 3 SG, 'tense' 3: *audiebat*; 2 PL, 'tense' 3: *audiebatis*. Understand what you've done – you've identified 'tense' and person/number morphemes. 'Tense' 4, ordered like the others, has the forms *audiam*, *audias*, *audiat*, *audiamus*, *audiatis*, *audiant*. What is the 'Tense' 4 marker? (It's *-a-*.)

2.7   For *traithe*: present indicative 2 SG *tu trai*, 3 SG *i'trait*, 2 PL *ou triyez*; present subjunctive 2 PL *ou traithêtes*, 3 PL *i'traient*. For *braithe*: present indicative 1 SG *j'brai*, 2 SG *tu brai*, 1 PL *j'briyons*, 2 PL *ou briyez*; present subjunctive 1 SG *j'braie*, 1 PL *j'braithêmes*, 3 PL *i'braient*.

2.8   *j'criyions*

2.9   *criyant*

2.10   *j'verrêmes*

2.11   *ou baivthêtes*

2.12   Five, defined by the ways in which their singular and plural suffixes pair off: *-o/-i, -a/-e, -a/-i, -e/-i, -o/-a*.

2.13   TO BE.

2.14   Noun: *smell, smells*; perhaps *smell's, smells'* (see Discussion earlier in this Unit). Verb: *smell, smells, smelling, smelt* or *smelled* (remember that some of these may have more than one grammatical meaning.)

2.15   (a) Seven lexemes, HAVE in two forms; (b) Eight lexemes, HALF in two forms; (c) Nine lexemes (surely the two STANDs are different lexemes?); (d) Ten lexemes, BE in two forms (one repeated). I have assumed I and MY are distinct lexemes, but you could argue they're not; (e) Fourteen lexemes, no lexeme in more than one form. LIKE appears as the distinct lexemes which are a noun, verb and preposition in that order; it also appears as a morpheme within DISLIKE. The LIKEs are all unalike.

3.1 Try SCISSORS, SUDS, TROUSERS, (THE) SPLITS, MEASLES and so on.

3.2 (a) Try PROTECTOR, CONFESSOR, DIRECTOR, VENDOR, SAILOR, CONTRACTOR and so on; (b) RESISTOR, CONNECTOR and others with -AT(E) like ESCALATOR, RADIATOR etc.; (c) TAILOR, DOCTOR, DONOR, SPONSOR, JUROR and so on.

3.3 The only grammatical morphemes are *-ing* (see Discussion), *-ed* (see Discussion), *-er*, *-est* and *-i*.

3.4   →

**UNIT 3
LEXICAL AND
GRAMMATICAL
MORPHOLOGY**

3.5

lingu-ist	util-ize	arrog-ant	alacr-ity	bi-ology
terr-ify	loc-ation/	mechan-ic	demo-crat	medit-ate
	locat(e)-ion			

3.6 Make a list of some relevant other words. The best evidence is RECURRENCE of the element in different words with essentially the same meaning or function.

3.7 Make a list of some relevant other words, as with Exercise 3.6. Remember that the meaning of the element should be similar – or preferably identical – in every word on your list.

3.8 You find *-monger* in a range of words like IRON-, FISH-, SCARE-, RUMOURMONGER, sufficient to suggest it means 'supplier (of)'. *-sume* appears in ASSUME, PRESUME, CONSUME with no obvious shared nucleus of meaning: not a separate morpheme. Likewise for *-ject* in PROJECT, INJECT, OBJECT as verbs. The historical meanings of 'take' and 'throw' are hard to recover from these. Those with knowledge of Latin will find it easier to recover them – they may see the English words as clearly based on the notions of taking and throwing.

3.9 Suggested meanings: PORNO- 'sexually explicit and seedy or shocking', BOV- 'cattle', MEDIC- 'to do with the healing arts', GER- 'old person', HORR- 'to do with fear and loathing', HISTO- 'tissue', LEUCO- 'white', ANDR- 'man', REGUL- 'rule', THEO- 'god'.

3.10 Suggested meanings: *auto-* 'self', *giga-* '10^9', *milli-* 'one-thousandth', *hemi-* 'half', *biblio-* 'book', *cruci-* 'cross', *tele-* historically 'far', but much harder to pin down now – perhaps 'channel or medium of communication' with a hint of long distance, *peri-* 'round about (the time of)', *manu-* 'by hand'. Notice that the words expressing these meanings can't necessarily just be slipped into the structure of the words you're examining. The more confident you are of the meaning, the more words the morpheme probably appears in.

3.11 Respectively 'fear of hearts', 'removal of the heart'; 'love of women', 'androgyny' (but the other way round), 'rule by women'; 'inspection of water with an optical instrument', 'measurement of water'.

UNIT 4 ROOTS, BASES, STEMS AND OTHER STRUCTURAL THINGS

4.1 HYMN, BREAK, SANE, MAJOR, GRAND, HUMAN, BREAK, LINK, BOARD, NEW

4.2 KNOW, TAINT, HEAT, SUFFER, BRAIN, ACT, DISCOVER (ARGUABLY), INHERIT, MINISTER, NORM

4.3 -TH, -AGE, -ABLE, -ITY, EN-, DIS- OR -ION (WHY?), -IZE, -Y, -Y, -ANT, PRE-, -ERY

4.4 →

4.5 LAY-ER, ACT-IVE, TRUTH-FUL (all complex themselves)

4.6 -s in *bathrooms*, -*(e)d* in *manhandled* if it's a verb-form such as 'past tense of MANHANDLE', and -*en* in *browbeaten* from the verb BROWBEAT.

4.7 TRUTHFULNESS

4.8 GASTRITIS, SQUEAMISH, LUDICROUS. You could make a case for AGRICULTURE if you believe it doesn't contain CULTURE.

4.9 You can tell by the grammatical morphemes that they take; cf. Exercise 2.14, and note *love-s, prepare-(e)d, review-ed, requisition-ed*. Also, of course, by the structure of the phrases they occur in, which is a matter of SYNTAX.

4.10 The main differentiating factor is STRESS, that is the degree of prominence of one syllable over the other; usually this means relative loudness. If the stressed syllable is the first, the word is a noun (CÓNVICT); if it's the second, it's a verb (CONVÍCT).

4.11 For instance DESPAIR, COMMAND, REVIEW, COLLAPSE, DELAY, COMFORT; ABSTRACT, CONFLICT, INCLINE, UPSET, TORMENT, PROGRESS. Note that there are subtle differences of pronunciation in the vowels of the last set depending on which lexical category they belong to.

4.12 They are all compounds except ISLAND and SISTERHOOD. The head is the second element except in LOCKJAW (see Exercise 4.13), SLEEPOVER, BLACKOUT and SIT-IN.

4.13 The exocentric ones are LOCKJAW ('disease which locks the jaw'), LIGHTWEIGHT ('a lightweight person'), EVERGREEN (if a noun, not an adjective, 'an evergreen tree'), SHORTCRUST (if an adjective, as in 'shortcrust pastry').

4.14 Those with independent bases are ACTOR-PRODUCER and GREY-GREEN; possibly also INTO, but since motion is the dominant idea you could treat INTO as a sort of TO.

5.1 For example BOOKMAKER, BOOKSHOP, BOOK TOKEN, BOOKBINDER, BOOKCASE, BOOKPLATE; HANDBOOK, STUD-BOOK, MATCHBOOK, EXERCISE BOOK, PRAYER-BOOK, YEARBOOK.

Notice the stress pattern of BOOK TOKEN and EXERCISE BOOK; they are compounds.

UNIT 5
COMPOUND
AND
COMPLEX
BASES

5.2 All these are [noun + noun] compounds of which the second noun is the head. Broadly, each compound noun in this list has a meaning related to 'noun 2 is for noun 1', for example 'the box is for matches', 'the brush is for hair'; or in some instances 'there is noun 2 for noun 1', such as 'there is room for legs'. The implied grammatical meaning of the first element – for instance singular or plural number – doesn't matter. FOOTBALL STADIUM has a first element which is itself compound.

5.3 DEATH-DEFYING: the type is 'adjective consisting of [noun + verb in -*ing*]', meaning 'which verbs the noun', here 'which defies death'. TOWN PLANNING: a [noun 1 + noun 2] compound noun, meaning roughly 'noun 2 of noun 1'. CHURCHGOER is '[noun + noun consisting of a verb with -*er* suffix]', meaning 'performer of the activity of the verb in the second noun in some relation to the first'. SHOW-STOPPER is similar. Return to the text for discussion of these two. ROCKING CHAIR is arguably a compound noun consisting of [noun in -*ing* derived from verb + noun] where the noun in -*ing* modifies the second noun in a sense like 'in which one (verb)s'. BOYFRIEND is a [noun 1 + noun 2] compound with the general meaning 'noun 2 which is/consists of (a) noun 1'; it has an additional or specific meaning of the type 'lover', of course. Further examples are: GODFEARING, LIFEGIVING, SELF-BASTING; BOOK-KEEPING, TIME-WASTING, SOUL-SEARCHING; WOOD-CARVER, BUS-DRIVER, SHEEP-SHEARER; SWIM-MING POOL, LIVING ROOM, POTTING SHED; ELM-TREE, CREOLE LANGUAGE, INDICATOR LIGHT.

5.4 All are compounds except the following, which are complex because of affixation (affixes in capital letters): PRE-*war*, *week*-LY, *strong*-LY, *odd*-ITY, *weak*-NESS, *schmaltz*-Y, IL-*licit*, *Calvin*-ISM, *grammar*-IAN, UN-*quiet*, *home*-LESS, *woman*-HOOD.

5.5 These are example answers only. INTER-: no clear function in relation to lexical categories; -LY makes adjectives from nouns (relating to a period of recurrence – WEEKLY) or from other adjectives (often denoting bodily states – a WEAKLY *lamb*), and adverbs from adjectives (*he smiled* WEAKLY); -EST makes the superlative of adjectives (no class-change, therefore); ARCH- makes a noun from a noun (ARCH-VILLAIN) with a kind of intensification or promotion of what it denotes – effectively no function in relation to classes; -OUS makes adjectives denoting possession of an attribute or quality named by the bound lexical morpheme (FERROUS) or noun (PERILOUS) to which it is attached; -AGE makes nouns from verbs with the meaning 'thing produced by the action named' (PACKAGE) or 'action itself' (SPILLAGE), or from nouns, with the meaning 'place' (ORPHANAGE); MONO-: no clear function; -ANT makes adjectives denoting the existence of a state named by a verb (EXPECTANT) and -ER makes nouns from verbs with the sense 'performer' (TRAINER) or 'instrument' (BOILER).

5.6 At least -LY, -AGE and -ER.

5.7 Prefixes in English are not class-changing.

5.8 BLOND(E) is an adjective; the suffix -EN makes a verb (cf. BLACKEN); the -ER is as in Exercise 5.5.

5.9 (SULPH)-ITE, (ISO-)MER, EXTRA(-MURAL), POLY (-VALENT), AMBI (-DEXTROUS), (DINO-)SAUR. And how about -EME in linguistics?

5.10 You've done enough to work these out for yourself – have some confidence!

6.1 *Geliyor-* 'come', *-u-* '1st person', *-m* '1st person singular', *-sun* '2nd person', 3rd person singular is unmarked, *-z* '1st person plural', *-uz* '2nd person plural', *-lar* '3rd person plural'. You could also extract an *-uz* meaning 'non-3rd person plural', but that would mean treating the *-um* of 'I am coming' differently – work out how.

6.2 The analysis remains unchanged except that '2nd person' is *-n* and 'first person plural' is *-k*.

6.3 (a) *-du*; (b) You have no alternative but to say that it's either *-sun* or *-n*, depending on the tense of the verb.

6.4 *-m-*. 'You (plural) were not coming' is *gelmiyordunuz*.

6.5 *-ecek*. This blows the gaff: the *-iyor* we met earlier is clearly not part of the stem.

6.6 Add *-ecek* to the stem *gel-*.

6.7 *-ir*. Add this to the stem *gel-*.

6.8 It's like English BE + -ING, technically called the 'continuous aspect'.

6.9 *gelirdim*, *gelirdin*, etc. You will probably have put *gelirdum*, *gelirdun*, etc. That is not unreasonable – give yourself a mark! Whether *-u-* or *-i-* appears in the final suffix usually depends on the vowel that precedes it. For those who have done some phonetics, this is vowel harmony. For similar reasons, '3rd person plural' is *gelirdiler* not *-lar*.

**UNIT 6
IDENTIFYING
GRAMMATICAL
MORPHEMES**

6.10 Allowing for vowel-harmony, Turkish still has different suffixes for '2nd person' and '1st person plural' depending on tense (non-past versus past).

6.11 'come' is *veni-*; the affixes, one in each verb-form, carry the person and number meanings. Perhaps you could claim *-s* is '2nd person' and *-t* '3rd person'.

6.12 The most economical solution is *-eba*.

6.13 We now have variants for '1st person singular': *-o* and *-m*; and for '3rd person plural': *-unt* and *-nt*.

6.14 *-s*

6.15 Some suffixes are special to this tense-form; others are related but require stem-augments individual to each word-form (see **Unit 7**).

6.16 *-ba*, not *-eba* as decided in Exercise 6.12.

6.17 The stem is arguably everything before the *-ba*, but the vowel-letter immediately before it varies according to the class of verb.

6.18 Either *-o* or *-m*. Which of these appears depends on which tense the verb shows. This is like what happens with the Turkish marker of '1st person plural'.

6.19 Turkish *-lar* '3rd person, plural number'; Latin *-o* '1st person, singular, certain tenses'.

6.20 The *-(e)s* suffix means all of these things: person (3rd; 1st and 2nd verbs don't have it), number (singular; plural verbs don't have the suffix), and tense (present; past verbs have a different marker).

6.21 Direct: *-l* 'past tense'. Cumulative: all the rest.

UNIT 7
WHERE TO FIX
AFFIXES

7.1 No.

7.2 *agor-*

7.3 Take the first consonant (if there is one) and vowel, and make a copy of them as a prefix. It helps to treat words beginning with a vowel as if they began with a ? (a glottal stop, like the Cockney 't' in *later*).

7.4 It is as if the stems are of the shape such as *p-X-usi*, where the *X* is a slot sitting waiting to receive any infix required by the grammar. The infix goes after the first consonant of the stem.

7.5   The patterns *CuCuuC*, *CaCaaCiC*, which are patterns of infixed vowels, are markers of the plural, whatever consonant is represented by *C*.

7.6   *quṣuur, bunuuk, funuun; zawaabiʕ, kanaayis, madaaris.*

7.7   *incumbent, recumbent, cubicle, succubus*; the missing form of 'leave' is *linquo*.

7.8   Prefixes: *ni-* '1st person singular', *ti-* '2nd person singular' and '1st person plural', *an-* '2nd person plural'. Suffixes: *-ni* 'continuous', *-s* 'future', *-ya* 'past', *-h* 'plural'. Note that *-yah* is two successive suffixes, not an infix and a suffix; the *-ya* isn't actually inside any other morpheme.

7.9   *ticho:cani, nicho:caya, cho:cas, ancho:cash* (this last on the evidence presented).

7.10   A type of reduplicative prefixation, and suffix-replacement. The suffix of the singular, which is translatable approximately as 'it is', has been marked off for you by a hyphen. Notice that 'mountain' is of the animate gender in Nahuatl.

7.11   *o:oce:loh* and *-po:po:chtin* (though you can't actually tell what suffix to use).

7.12   Two, *-t-* and *-it-*.

7.13   On this evidence, by infixation before the final vowel of the stem.

7.14   An infix meaning 'plural'.

7.15   A prefix meaning '1st person'.

7.16   An infix *-t-* placed after *-la-* (the morpheme identified in Exercise 7.14) in any word-form where that appears.

7.17   *ge-* is not chosen if there is already a prefix.

7.18   Because they are different forms of the same verb, not different verbs and still less members of different lexical categories altogether.

7.19   By ablaut – the vowel of the first syllable is lengthened (or doubled).

UNIT 8
WORD-FORMATION BY REDUCTION

8.1   *giro, cello, PIN, ID, fax, ecu/ECU, BSE, vegeburger/ veggieburger*

8.2   Various sorts of filled bread rolls were called generically *burger*.

8.3   It's from *fanatic*.

8.4   *fridge*: procope and apocope from *refrigerator*; *movie*: apocope from *moving picture*, and extension by suffix; *Spurs*: procope from (*Tottenham*) *Hotspur*, and plural suffixation; *Gers*: procope from (*Glasgow*) *Rangers*; *con-man*: con by apocope from *confidence(-trickster)*; *cute* by procope from *acute*; *cyborg* by double apocope from *cybernetic organism*; *electrocute* by apocope of *electric* and apocope of *execute*, with an augment -*o*- on the first base; *Lambo* by apocope from *Lamborghini*; *Oz* by apocope from *Australia*; *detox* by apocope from *detoxification*, and *dis* from *disrespect*; *Becky* like *fridge*; *europhile*: first element by apocope from *Europe(an)*, used as a bound lexical morpheme; *loony*: by apocope from *lunatic* and suffixation; *rugger* thus from *rugby*; *Mountie* like *loony* from *mounted police(man)*; *Herts* by double apocope from *Hertford* and *shire*, pronounced as a single word; *coke* by apocope from either *Coca-Cola* or *cocaine*; *cami-knickers* by apocope of the first element *camisole*; *mums* by procope from *chrysanthemums*; *Tanzania* by apocope of *Tanganyika* and *Zanzibar*, formed into a single unit and suffixed; *alco-pop* by apocope of *alcohol* and then like *europhile*. Several of the outcomes have been re-spelt, e.g. *Oz* and *coke*, and others have a pronunciation which is strictly not quite that of the abbreviated form, such as *Lambo*, *Oz*.

8.5   breath + analyser; motor + hotel; transfer + resistor; guess + estimate; parachute + trooper; channel + tunnel; travel + escalator. Weaker: *breathalyser, guesstimate, paratrooper, travelator*; stronger: *motel, transistor, Chunnel*.

8.6   *Guesstimate*, with /es/ shared by both originals.

8.7   Acronyms: *VAT, WASP, Fiat*; initialisms: *VAT, REM, UB(40), DOA, BMW*.

8.8   *HRT, ME, IRA, TLC, AC/DC*: initialisms; *nimby, EFTPOS, ROM*: acronyms; *camcorder*: strong blend; *parascending*: blend (whether weak or strong depends on how you interpret the second *a*); *acupressure, docudrama*: weak blends; *pro-am*: double apocope compound; *BSc*: sort of initialism but like *PhD* or *ID* above.

8.9   *Stan*, *Pete* and *Mike*: simple apocope (*Mike* in pronunciation); *Chas*: pronounced written form of abbreviation, but also like two of the following names; *Del, Daz, Gaz*: apocope and substitution of some consonant for /r/; *Tony*: originally procope, relation to modern pronunciation of *Anthony* with stressed *An*- more problematic; *Mick*: probably from spelling apocope; *Sly*: eccentric from adjustment to spelling after apocope; *Sally, Mally*: like *Del* and suffixed; *Ginny*:

procope and apocope; *Katie*: now eccentric from older pronunciation of *Catherine* – originally apocope and suffixation; *Maggie, Meg, Frankie*: apocope with pronunciation adjustment; *Gail*: procope.

8.10 Over to you!

8.11 (a) phrases consisting of adjective + noun; (b) two: compound consisting of apocopated versions of both words, and weak blend (where the second word is intact).

8.12 The nearest parallels are the *pro-am* and *docudrama* types.

8.13 The first type is what I called a double apocope compound in answer to Exercise 8.8. It's a sort of blend. The second type is weak blending.

9.1 *shepherd/sheep, cone/conic, pig/piggy, divide/division, long/ length, deceive/deception, keep/kept*; remember only one morpheme in each of these words shows allomorphy. *Sieve/sieved* and *drive/driven* also show allomorphy, if you accept that the suffixes are *-ed* and *-en*; that yields the allomorphs *sieve/siev-* and *drive/driv-*.

9.2 The alternations can be recovered from the list of words in the answer to Exercise 9.1: *shep-/sheep, cone/con-, pig/pigg-, divide/ divis-*, and so on.

9.3 All of them; cf. *tone/tonic, twig/twiggy, deride/derision, strong/strength, receive/reception*; that in *shepherd/sheep* is the same as that in *kept/keep*.

9.4 In word-final position you find *-e*, and elsewhere the relevant base has no *-e*. Note that this is a generally valid rule.

9.5 The allomorph *-es* occurs after final *-(t)ch, -s* and *-sh*, and after final single *-o*. Adding further data will show that the last of these is not regular; cf. *pianos, radios*. Former US Vice-President Dan Quayle famously illustrated the problem that this gives rise to by 'correcting' a schoolchild's spelling of the singular to *potatoe*.

9.6 The second morpheme in each word in the left-hand column ends in *-y* when final in the word, but in *-i-* when another suffix is added.

9.7 →

9.8 →

9.9 In word-final position you find *-f*, and before the plural suffix *-ve*.

UNIT 9
ALLOMORPHY:
BOOKS WITH
MORE THAN
ONE COVER

9.10 The most likely different forms are *dreamed*, *burned*, *learned*, *spelled*, *spoiled*, *kneeled*, *leaped*, *wreaked*, *beseeched*, *bereaved*, *formulas*, *indexes*, *brothers* and *pronounciation* (look at that last one closely!). The bases before the final affix – mostly stems before a grammatical affix – show allomorphy in the original data-set, but not in the list just given.

9.11 *an* is used before a word beginning with a vowel letter, but with some exceptions that we return to, such as *a use* (not *an use*).

9.12 All of them except *pig/pigg-*.

9.13 It's tidier. You get /iz/ after sibilants, /z/ after voiced sounds except sibilants and /s/ after voiceless sounds except sibilants.

9.14 /h/ is absent for them at the beginning of a word in an unstressed syllable; such words thus begin with a vowel and are preceded by *an*, not *a*. (cf. Exercise 9.11.)

9.15 Adding the adjective-forming suffix -IC to the base in the left-hand column has the effect of attracting the word-stress – the greatest prominence in the word – to the syllable immediately before the -IC.

9.16 *Arábic*. This is the form used by many foreign speakers of English, quite consistently with the general rule.

9.17 The first three don't contain the suffix -IC. The last three don't contain a free base as all others in the exercise do. This may be relevant.

UNIT 10 ALLOMORPHY IN OTHER LANGUAGES

10.1 The *en-* prefix appears in different forms according to the first consonant of the stem.

10.2 The form *-tli* is used where the stem of the noun ends in a consonant, and *-tl* where it ends in a vowel, i.e. the alternation is governed solely by pronunciation factors. The form *-li* is used solely where there is a preceding consonant (therefore the form of the suffix is not *-l*), and that consonant is /l/. Again, the governing factor is purely to do with pronunciation.

10.3 Generally: after a nasal consonant the form of the article is /na/, after other consonants /la/, after a front vowel /ja/, after a nasal vowel /ã/ and after other vowels /a/. Note what happens after a nasal front vowel, in 'way', and after a consonant preceded by a nasal vowel, in 'lie'.

10.4 Reading across, /la/, /na/, /na/, /a/, /ã/, /a/ respectively.

10.5   The upper group, with *-nak*, *-ól*, have stems whose last vowel is *o*, *a*, *á*. These are non-front vowels. The lower group, with *-nek*, *-ől*, have stems whose last vowel is *ö*, *e*. These are front vowels. Vowel harmony dictates the choice of suffix allomorph.

10.6   If there are both non-front and front vowels in the same stem, the back vowel dictates the choice of suffix allomorph.

10.7   The words for 'aim' and 'bridge' take a suffix allomorph which is not the expected one. They must be treated as exceptions.

10.8   →

10.9   *Barátoknak, feleségtől.*

10.10   *Házról, kertről, hídról.*

10.11   This is problematic. Monosyllables take *-heit*. Adjectives with suffixes that are a full syllable take *-keit*.

10.12   Obviously the form *l'* is chosen in response to the requirements of pronunciation. It's chosen when the following word (in each of these instances a noun) begins with a vowel.

10.13   →

10.14   These pairs show allomorphy of the stem: *kubúnth-/kubúnt-, kutháβ-/kutháv-, kuwɔp-/kuwɔf-*. The causative suffix is discussed in the text.

10.15   Morphological class.

10.16   Right! No principle at all.

TECHNICAL TERMS INDEX

The page indicated is the one on which the term is introduced or defined

LANGUAGE INDEX